THE NARCISSIST...
then me!

AVERY CHARLES

To My Heavenly Mum

If not for you, I would not exist. The humblest, authentic soul with love that spread her angel wings so high. My guardian angel who shines love and light on all her girls.

You gave me the strength to help all powerful survivors to make them an army of warriors: the ultimate epiphany of humanity at its best.

You made me who I am today... It's taken a while to get there, but for that journey, I am thankful.

Forever Grateful

X

"In the pursuit of power, you may silence voices, shatter spirits, and leave scars that endure long after your control fades–the erosion of the soul, the theft of self-worth, and the silencing of dreams. But true strength lies not within domination but with compassion, empathy, and the ability to uplift others without diminishing their light."

"In your shadows, I withered the storm of your ego, but through the darkness, I discovered my resilience, strength, and the unwavering light of my true self. Break the cycle of abuse, for in healing the wounds you inflict, and you liberate not only others but also yourself, finding the strength to be the person you were meant to be."

Avery Charles

ABOUT THE AUTHOR

Meet Avery Charles, a wonderful woman who has overcome emotional abuse and is now helping others do the same! Originally from a small town in Northern England, Avery has gained a wealth of knowledge about narcissism and narcissistic abuse from her own experiences and those of others who have been through it. She believes that only those who have experienced this kind of trauma can truly understand it and help others heal from it. Avery is passionate about helping other survivors thrive and see their worth and value, and she's determined to make a difference in the world!

Avery's experience as a survivor has enabled her to assist others in overcoming the traumatic challenges they have confronted. She was inspired to educate others about the harsh realities of living in a delusional state after writing her personal journal. Now, she wants everyone to know that a joyful, truthful, and healthy life is within reach and that you can find your way out of the darkness. Remember, even though the world is spinning so fast, you don't have to live deep in the lonely!

Avery Charles' mission in authoring these helpful books is mainly to share her own experiences and offer valuable guidance on coping with emotional abuse. Through her writing, she wants her readers to feel supported, empowered and understood. Whether you're feeling alone, struggling with symptoms, or questioning your self-worth, Avery's got your back. Her books are perfect for anyone looking to take control of their life and achieve a sense of freedom. So, if you're ready to improve your relationships and emotional intelligence, join Avery's community of men and women who are on the same journey as you!

Here's Avery's message for you: always feel confident, cultivate positive habits, and be more mindful. Her book is full of tools to help you recognize emotional abuse, understand those awful feelings of worthlessness and isolation, and heal from them. You will also find actionable solutions for becoming a stronger, more resilient person. Remember, you have the power to take control of your own life and be your best self!

CONTENTS

About the Author...5

Introduction...1

Chapter 1: *Recognizing Narcissism* 7

Chapter 2: *Understanding Narcissistic Personality Disorder* 27

Chapter 3: *The Moment You Realize* 41

Chapter 4: *Types of Narcissism* 55

Chapter 5: *Signs and Symptoms of Narcissistic Abuse*................63

Chapter 6: *The Dark Triad*.......................................75

Chapter 7: *Narcissistic Tactics*.................................89

Chapter 8: *Narcissists Splitting* 107

Chapter 9: *Self-Love*.. 121

Chapter 10: *The Survivors Journey* 137

Chapter 11: *Physical and Mental Effects of Narcissistic Abuse* .. 149

Chapter 12: *The Road to Healing* 161

Chapter 13: *Reality & Truths* 169

Conclusion 177

Resources 182

INTRODUCTION

Have you ever noticed how much we love taking selfies and sharing them online? It's become a big part of our culture and daily routine. But have you ever heard someone say, "Oh, that person is such a narcissist!"? We tend to use that word to describe someone who seems really into themselves. But, is that really what narcissism means? Can we really just throw that term around casually?

Before we explore what narcissism is, let's talk about where the term comes from.

The word "narcissism" wasn't always a psychoanalytic term! It originated from a story in a book called Metamorphoses written by a Roman poet named Ovid. It originated from a story in a book called Metamorphoses written by a Roman poet named Ovid in the first century. The story is about a man named Narcissus and a woman named Echo. It's a fascinating mythical tale that offers valuable insights into human nature. You see, extreme self-love, or narcissism, can have a negative impact on your life and those around you. Since narcissists are always focused on themselves, everything else seems insignificant or even worthless to them. But did you know that sometimes the opposite can also be true?

It's not just self-obsession that can be unhealthy, but codependency – when you rely on someone else too much – can also be quite harmful. It's important to remember to take care of yourself and not neglect your own needs while trying to please others. In fact, the classic tale we just talked about describes Echo exactly this way. On the other hand, Narcissus is a character from ancient Greek mythology who is the most famous for falling head over heels in love with his own reflection! That, too, to the point where he couldn't tear himself away and ended up dying of hunger and thirst. Sounds absolutely crazy, right?

And then, this female nymph named Echo gets involved, falls in love with him, and of course, she gets rejected. The story essentially shows how these two extremes can often find their way into relationships. The lesson we can take from Echo and Narcissus is to strive to find balance in our lives, yet you will still find both extremes in people around you to this day...

That's how the term "Narcissism" came to be what it is today. The story of Narcissus still holds true in today's understanding of narcissism. It's a personality trait that can range from self-importance to extreme self-absorption, and in some cases, indicate a disorder called Narcissistic Personality Disorder (NPD). And one of the key signs of NPD is a sense of superiority, thinking that you are better than everyone else, and feeling entitled. Those with NPD usually have highly inflated levels of self-esteem but also require constant praise and admiration.

Imagine living with a person who only believes in their own worth, who only ever treats themselves as human beings, for whom no one else matters... If you are reading this, you probably don't have to imagine it. Even if it is a loved one who's going or has gone through narcissistic abuse, it's easy to see the damage such a relationship can cause. Living with a narcissist can drain you to the point that you lose your own self.

Let me tell you about the time I met my supposed 'soulmate.' I thought I found 'the one' in a heartbeat. We clicked right away, and it was like looking into a mirror – we were so similar in so many ways. The love I felt was like nothing I had ever felt before. It was genuine and raw. As a couple, we were so caring, trustworthy, and honest with each other. From the moment I met him, my heart overflowed with love for him. He was my soulmate, and I cherished the idea of spending our lives together, growing old, and creating memories.

Until he wasn't.

Suddenly, he was gone. The man I saw my future with had vanished. And I was left with nothing but an aching feeling of emptiness and confusion. Where had he gone? The man who loved me just as much as I loved him?

And just like that, everything came crashing down.

While there are always kind-hearted people in this world, sometimes it can be hard to know what's really going on behind closed doors or beneath a smile. You may think you know this person and love them with all your heart before you realize who they actually are. And by that time, it's probably too late. Sometimes, it's easy to notice when someone is mistreating you, abusing you, or manipulating you. However, there are times when it's not so obvious and can be quite sneaky, which is sadly far more common. If we knew we were getting involved with a narcissist, wouldn't we just back off from the beginning?

Most narcissists are really covert and clever when it comes to trapping their victims. This can leave you feeling unsure if what you experienced actually happened or if you're just being sensitive. These doubts and self-blame are all part of a harmful cycle of manipulation caused by narcissistic abuse. Sadly, this type of behavior can occur in any relationship, whether with a narcissistic family member, friend, partner, or even a boss. And by the time you realize where you are and what has happened to you, you're in too deep. Help is always available, but not around you...

It's truly heartbreaking to see someone pushed to the brink of feeling like they have no way out. I've been to some dark places myself, and that feeling of being lost is one of the worst kinds of mental torture. It takes a lot of courage to speak up, but unfortunately, some people just don't understand and instead make you feel like you're doing something wrong. It's tough when the people you thought were your friends are questionable. Life can be challenging, and sadly, people can be even crueler, but remember, life is a gift. It's up to you to take charge of your own happiness and make the most of every moment.

It's wonderful that each and every one of us has a unique voice and perspective, and I always encourage my children to speak up and share their opinions. Even if we don't always agree with one another, it's essential to treat each other with kindness and respect. Unfortunately, sometimes we can fall into the trap of judging others without truly understanding their experiences. Let's focus on living our lives to the fullest and supporting each other along the way!

No matter what you have gone through, or even if you're still going through it, let's celebrate the fact that you've recognized and acknowledged the abuse you are or have been subjected to. That's all on you, and trust me when I say that's the bravest thing you can do. Love always begins with self-love. Realizing your own worth is always the first step to healing from any kind of trauma or abuse. And whether you're here to heal from it or escape, know that you're at the right place. You are not alone. You are amazing. You can do it.

It's almost unbelievable to think about how far I've come in my own journey to finding inner peace and happiness. Life can be full of unexpected twists and turns, but I've learned to embrace the journey no matter what. This past year has been especially challenging for me, filled with emotional ups and downs that have left me feeling drained. Despite experiencing some major losses, I've managed to find strength and hope in the midst of grief. It's been a wild ride, but I'm grateful for all the lessons I've learned along the way. And now I want you to know you can do the same!

I found it hard to crack a smile from the inside out for the longest time. I couldn't see myself clearly, and sometimes, I didn't even like the person I saw. Being stuck in a life that doesn't bring you joy can leave you feeling lost and unwell. But you know what the key to true happiness is? It's all about having a wholesome relationship built on love, trust, respect, loyalty, and kindness. Knowing that you're genuinely loved and waking up feeling grateful every day is beautiful. So, my dear friend, don't settle for anything less than fulfillment. Enjoy your life to the fullest because you never know when it'll be your last.

Life is an adventure full of ups and downs, but every experience teaches us something valuable. It can be tough when those closest to us let us down, but remember that your well-being is the most important thing. Don't be afraid to seek happiness and contentment elsewhere if someone brings you down. You are capable of rising above any challenge and thriving as your authentic self. Stay positive because the universe has a way of rewarding us for our optimism. I truly believe that the people we meet along the way are there for a reason, whether for a brief moment or a lifetime. It's all part of the journey!

CHAPTER 1:

RECOGNIZING NARCISSISM

Have you ever known someone who just can't seem to think of anyone but themselves? We all have moments of self-absorption, but true narcissists take it to the next level. They often ignore the needs and feelings of those around them, and they don't even realize how their behavior affects others. So, how exactly do you recognize a narcissist?

Let's face it, figuring out if someone is a narcissist can be a bit of a puzzle. But don't worry, you don't need a fancy medical test or high-tech gadget to solve it. While there's no foolproof method, some handy inventories and scales can help you sort things out. So take a deep breath, relax, and let's get to the bottom of this together!

Most narcissists are:

Self-Absorbed

Suppose you have a coworker named Adam. Whenever there is a company dinner, he's the type of person who is always eager to take what he wants without considering whether there's enough left for everyone else. Is he a narcissist? Or is he just really enthusiastic about trying new foods? When it comes to small talk, he shares stories about his successes at work and his accomplishments all the time. Is he bragging out of self-centeredness, or is he just trying to make a good impression?

The question is, how do you find out if a person is just self-absorbed or a narcissist? While it's true that full-blown narcissists tend to be self-absorbed, let's not mistake all self-centered people for being narcissistic. Did you know that many experts believe that narcissism, like other mental health concerns, exists on a spectrum?

Let's talk about attention and family dynamics for a moment. You see, quite a few people in this world tend to focus on themselves more than others. It's often said that those who were showered with attention as children or lacked proper guidance may develop self-centered tendencies. It's also true that only children often receive a lot of attention from their families, which can make them seem more self-absorbed than others. After all, they didn't have to deal with sharing or feeling like things were unfair with siblings. But how much parents spoil or enable their only child can also impact their level of self-centeredness.

Now, when it comes to self-focus, there's a spectrum to consider. And narcissists and self-absorbed people tend to be even in this regard. Here, we have to notice how differently both these groups react to criticism. For example, if Adam's partner points out something he's doing that bothers them, he could take it to heart and even try to work on changing his behavior, given that he is a self-absorbed person. However, if Adam is a narcissist, he will brush it off or even get upset because he feels criticized.

Remember that even if some narcissists try to accommodate, it may not be genuine and won't necessarily lead to a lasting change in their behavior!

A lesser-known fact is that even those who tend to focus on themselves can still have empathy. On the other hand, narcissists might try to pretend they care about others, but in reality, they view them as nothing more than mere pawns in their own world. A self-absorbed person who is **not** a narcissist does value their own needs and desires that they might even seek validation from others and often finds a way to share their experiences when they feel overlooked or undervalued. While they may sometimes dominate conversations with their personal anecdotes, they can actively listen to others and engage in meaningful dialogue – unlike narcissists.

Recognizing the difference between a self-absorbed person and a true narcissist is important. While both may crave attention, a narcissist takes it to the extreme by not truly listening to others and constantly shifting the focus back to themselves and their achievements. On the other hand, a self-centered person may simply be asking for recognition and validation. Moreover, a person who prioritizes their own needs and desires tends to hold strong moral beliefs, such as respecting the rules of society and being faithful to their partners. These individuals still possess empathy and consideration for others. However, those who exhibit narcissistic traits believe themselves to be exceptional and above the rules that apply to everyone else. They may find ways to justify cutting in line or betraying their partner and then shift the blame onto others when confronted.

Entitled

Isn't it interesting how some people can come across as incredibly charming and impressive, while others are just plain unpleasant? Similarly, narcissists can also appear to be very loving and caring at first. In fact, most of them actually put in effort to come across that way! It's only after spending some time with them that we come to realize the truth: everything always seems to revolve around them!

While, for a normal person, it's only natural to want to be respected, appreciated, and treated with consideration, narcissists seem to live in a different reality where they lack empathy and rely solely on their sense of superiority. It's a shame, really. Have you noticed how common it is for some people to adopt an entitled attitude without giving much thought to others? That really makes you think how many narcissists are just roaming around us.

If you've ever been in a relationship with a narcissist, you're probably familiar with how even the most generous and caring ones can become incredibly unreasonable during episodes of narcissistic entitlement. It can be extremely bewildering, hurtful, and even hazardous with how they behave and what they expect from you. It doesn't feel right, as this toxic behavior stems from an unhealthy and flawed mindset.

While it's true that everyone has different expectations regarding how they are treated, some people really do believe that they deserve special treatment from you or others. There are many situations in which this may come up. For example, a narcissist will feel upset if they are not the center of attention, even if someone else deserves recognition at a certain moment. They may also expect you to drop everything and prioritize their needs as soon as they become available, like they are the only person that matters or should matter to you. They could even demand that they be the only one receiving all of your affection or terms of endearment.

In some cases, they even want to have more control over aspects of your life than you're comfortable with. They often feel like they deserve to know who you're talking to and have access to your accounts and even your passwords. Sometimes, they behave in completely unacceptable ways, yet they feel entitled to do so. They won't ask you to do something for them, they will demand it be done. It's like your needs and wants don't even exist to them! These people feel a strong sense of entitlement, which can be really harmful to you. In other words, they are solely focused on what they want, without considering how it could impact those around them.

Don't ever forget that this behavior is not okay and you deserve to have boundaries in your relationships. The list of entitled behaviors can go on and on, but it's crucial to recognize them and stand up for yourself.

Demeaning

Have you ever chatted with someone who always seems to find fault with you, uses unkind words, and leaves you questioning your own thoughts? If you have, it's possible that you were in the company of a narcissist. These individuals tend to employ different approaches to keep their targets quiet, dominate talks, and evade; taking ownership of their behavior.

Some people can be really hurtful with their words. And those who struggle with narcissism even resort to name-calling to put others down. They might use words like "dumb", "stupid", or "foolish" to make you feel inferior. But that's not all! Some of them even use offensive language, including sexist or racist comments, to show their power over others. Just to feel good about themselves...

These narcissists also like to use gaslighting and emotional manipulation. It's not a fun thing to experience at all, which is why it's important to recognize when it's happening. These tactics are often used by narcissists who try to make their victims feel like their feelings and opinions don't matter. It's not okay to belittle someone or make them feel like they are too sensitive, no matter the situation. We all have valid feelings and should be able to express them without being blamed for creating problems that don't exist. But, again, narcissists don't care about you! They use these tactics to maintain power and control over someone, leaving the latter feeling confused, isolated, and vulnerable.

But did you know that narcissists who constantly belittle others might actually be struggling with their own insecurities, fears, and flaws? They might be afraid that their true selves will be exposed to those around them. By making hurtful comments, they try to reinforce their own sense of importance while hiding their own low self-esteem and self-worth. This explains why these individuals actively seek out ways to hurt others, in order to feel better about themselves. It's almost like an addiction for them, where seeing someone else hurt is what makes them feel good, or gives them a high. Of course, this behavior doesn't excuse them from any negative consequences that might arise from their actions.

Remember that a narcissist's hurtful actions toward you are never accidental. Sure, they may be struggling with their own deep-seated insecurities that they've carried with them since childhood, but these negative feelings can intensify over time, leading them to lash out and put you down to boost their self-worth. It's not about you, and it's about the feelings they're trying to hide from the world.

Remember to take care of yourself and surround yourself with positive and supportive people who truly value you. Always trust your gut and seek support if you ever feel like someone is trying to manipulate you.

Distrustful

When it comes to what makes a relationship successful, there are plenty of things to consider. But in my opinion, nothing beats the importance of trust. Without trust, no relationship can truly flourish. It's the foundation upon which other vital traits like respect, honesty, reliability, responsibility, and authenticity are built.

Dealing with narcissists can be a bit of a challenge, and it can become even more of a challenge when they are paranoid and distrustful. You'll often find them being suspicious of people and thinking that everyone is out to get them. There is no trust, no honesty, and nothing healthy in such a relationship. This can also be tied back to the fact that narcissists often face challenges with their inner workings. Their sense of integrity fluctuates, and they struggle with feelings of insecurity. Even their loyalty is only for their own personal gain. And because they possess a strong need for control, they are never mindful of others' needs and feelings, which makes it difficult to build mutual trust.

Some narcissists who struggle with emotional intelligence also have difficulty forming deep connections with others, but they often have a sharp mind when it comes to manipulating those around them. While they may understand the importance of trust and vulnerability in relationships, they are not able to fully commit to someone due to their emotional limitations. Instead, they engage in a one-sided relationship with the intention of taking advantage of their partner. Since they lack the ability to show vulnerability and trust, they may appear detached and aloof – this could also be in order to protect themselves from potential emotional harm.

Perfectionist

If someone has a tendency toward both perfectionism and narcissism, they may react to mistakes with aggression. This can result in completely disproportionate outbursts that can leave you feeling overwhelmed and demoralized. Imagine, for example, making a small spelling error on a document only to be publicly berated, fired, and humiliated by your narcissistic boss. In the same way, a parent could scold you in front of everyone for making a simple mistake or even for not living up to their expectations.

It's important to remember that in these situations, the narcissist will never take responsibility for their own mistakes. They may have a rigid, black-and-white way of thinking that exacerbates the problem. Let me put it this way – narcissistic perfectionists have a unique view of themselves. They see themselves as special and one-of-a-kind, and it's not unusual for them to hold those around them to impossibly high standards. Their perfectionism is not only limited to them, but they also expect others around them to be "perfect".

Now, this can make it challenging for them to work harmoniously with others. A narcissistic perfectionist would be the type of parent who wants their child to excel in a particular area, even if they don't expect the same level of perfection from anyone else. If you were to take a peek inside their mind, you'd notice how they always think unkind and judgmental thoughts about others. Yet, they also hold a high opinion of themselves, often thinking, "I'm great and flawless, and you're not."

While having high expectations of someone can be positive because that shows how highly they think of that person, when it is paired with a sense of entitlement and unrealistic demands, it can create a very negative dynamic. Narcissistic perfectionists also have a habit of blaming others for their problems instead of taking responsibility. It's never their fault. It's always your fault.

Superior

I'm sure you know or have met at least one person in your life who seems to think they're a cut above the rest. They might be suffering from a superiority complex, which means they have an attitude of superiority that masks their true feelings of inferiority and failure. And that's also what sets narcissists apart from the general population. But these narcissists who often come across as having high self-esteem could actually be the opposite! It's just an illusion they create to convince themselves that they're better than those around them despite feeling inferior deep down inside. This is also why they adopt unhealthy and toxic tactics to make their victims feel bad about themselves and their capabilities.

One way they try to make a good impression is by projecting an image of success that might not be true at all. This can involve things like dressing up in fancy clothes or driving a flashy car just to show others that they are "superior". These are simply tactics to deceive and manipulate others. Some of them even stretch the truth about their accomplishments as far as claiming their business is flourishing when it is not, or their busy schedule when they have a lot of extra time on their hands.

But, you know what? Sometimes, this behavior is unintentional, and these narcissists might not even realize they are doing it! They are just so used to acting in such a way, to lie and cheat their way out of situations that these acts become second nature to them. They just have to be superior, so they'll do anything to feel that way.

Unempathetic & Approval Seeking

People who possess a good amount of empathy are usually the ones who are always willing to lend a helping hand and show genuine concern for others. These people take pleasure in assisting others and make it a priority to do so. However, for narcissistic people, empathy is not something they can quite relate to. They have no drive to help others. Nevertheless, they might pretend to be kind and helpful to receive appreciation and admiration from others. This is what satisfies them the most: the affirmation that they are doing a good job, or that they are great.

When it comes to narcissism, it's important to understand that it's not just about having a big ego or being confident. Narcissists truly believe they are superior to others and deserve special treatment. This can lead to them constantly seeking attention, admiration, and praise from others, as they thrive on feeling important and special. And while it's always nice to see people doing good deeds, narcissists only do them to boost their public image.

They are specifically keen on their social status influence and they see acts of generosity as a way to appear noble and kind. They may donate their money or time to show that they "care," but the main goal is to gain public recognition. Although receiving acknowledgment for doing good deeds is perfectly normal, the true reward is in the act itself.

Narcissists do seem really confident but actually have fake self-esteem. They often base their worth on how they compare to others, and if they're not feeling superior, their confidence will crumble. And one way they try to boost themselves up is by being helpful and giving – it helps them feel like they're better than everyone else. They fake empathy and they act as if they care about you until you do something 'wrong.' Then, they just stop. They stop caring. In truth, they never did care about you or anyone else.

Unremorseful

Narcissists hardly, if ever, consider the impact of their actions on others. It's common for them to prioritize their own needs above others, even when expressing feelings of love. They don't care about you, so how can they ever feel bad about what they do to you? A lack of empathy is always followed by a lack of remorse, at least when it comes to dealing with a narcissist.

In healthy relationships, love is unconditional and based on a deep connection with the person themselves. However, in narcissistic relationships, love is merely transactional – they only want you around when you are meeting their needs. So, even if a narcissist claims that they truly love you, they are actually in love with the things you do for them. This means that their attachment to you is not as deep as it may seem. If you were to lose the qualities they value, they would easily and quickly lose interest and start showing their true feelings and personality. If, for example, you are going through a hard time, they will not only disregard your worries but also make you feel inferior without feeling remorseful for what they are doing or have done to you.

We all have our flaws and mistakes; sometimes, it can be tough to own up to them. But for narcissists, it can be even harder to acknowledge any shortcomings. They always focus solely on their inflated and superior view of themselves, using defense mechanisms to keep uncomfortable truths at bay. They never feel any guilt or shame, as their narcissistic defenses protect them from these emotions. This is also why they never see any reason to apologize or make amends, even if their behavior has hurt others. No matter how much they have wronged you, they will continue to blame you. Remember how it's never their fault?

Despite their unremorsefulness, it's not uncommon for narcissists to experience feelings of regret when they lose or let go of someone. But wait! I don't mean that in the way you're probably assuming. I mean that some narcissists may regret losing someone,

19

but they view others as possessions rather than individuals with their own emotions. While they may pretend to care about your feelings, the truth is that they are solely focused on their own needs and desires. So, they will only feel bad for letting you go if they need something from you.

Addictive

Just like how narcissists are too obsessed with themselves, they can also be addicted to certain substances like drugs and alcohol, and even to bad habits or people. When it comes to substance abuse, it can take advantage of their insecurities and some may even have a genetic susceptibility. Because narcissists often have to suffer from intense feelings of shame, they resort to alcohol or drugs in an attempt to solve the problem or distract themselves away from it. This kind of behavior can lead to a pattern of dependent behaviors that can have negative consequences.

There are a lot of similarities between narcissists and addicts. People with NPD (Narcissistic Personality Disorder – we'll talk about that in the next chapter) may also struggle with substance use disorders. They turn to substances as a way to numb or avoid negative emotions such as guilt, shame, and low self-esteem, considering they feel those in the first place. They could feel the need to hide these feelings to maintain their sense of superiority, and substance abuse can become a way of achieving that goal.

Unfortunately, the use of alcohol can exacerbate their narcissistic traits and make them even more negative and cruel.

While it may temporarily boost their sense of superiority, it can also lead to even more harmful behavior toward others – they generally show who they truly are under substance abuse.

Emotionally Detached

With all the lack of empathy, feelings of superiority, and entitled behavior, it's not surprising to learn that narcissists are also emotionally detached. All narcissists indeed struggle with emotional availability, but not everyone who may seem detached or distant is necessarily a narcissist.

Narcissists have difficulty connecting emotionally with others mostly because they don't trust others. They keep their emotional distance from others because they don't experience the same emotional rewards that most of us do when we share our thoughts and feelings with each other. Instead, they crave the excitement of being admired and infatuated with. They just want to overcome their deep insecurities, and showing their emotional side could do the opposite.

Did you know that people who struggle with emotional unavailability and those who are narcissistic often share a lack of empathetic traits? Still, there is a significant difference between the two. Emotionally unavailable individuals can still connect with others at some level and may try to see things from your perspective, even if they don't necessarily agree. They may even feel remorse or guilt for their actions and can work on improving their relationship skills. On the other hand, narcissists lack the core empathy necessary for creating lasting and loving connections.

How They Reveal Themselves

Since narcissists only care about themselves, and they can be tricky to deal with. While it's important to be aware of their behaviors, it's also crucial to remember that identifying them can help keep you and your loved ones safe. Now that we know what narcissism looks like let's talk about how narcissists unintentionally reveal themselves to you, including the signs you may miss or not look out for.

With this knowledge, you'll be able to steer clear of potentially harmful situations and avoid people who may not have your best interests at heart.

There's no doubt that narcissists are often incredibly charming, especially when you first meet them. They seem like they really have a way with people! They have a certain sense of confidence that allows them to come across however they want to others. But, if you observe closely, you will notice that they often feel a bit artificial or fake. That's how they're showing you they're a narcissist.

If we talk about a narcissist's ability to take charge of situations, it might sound like they're born leaders. But that's not true. They love having power and control to an unhealthy degree and often find themselves in positions of authority as a result. You might find yourself drawn to their natural leadership abilities, which can be quite impressive, but the same qualities will tear you down later!

Another way to spot a narcissist is to observe whether they love sharing their own stories and experiences. No matter what the discussion is about, a narcissist always has a way to add something about them to share, to divert all the attention to themselves, and have others sing their praises. They often get carried away with talking about themselves, but it's not always seen as unusual. Some might say they're eager to connect with others, but you can definitely tell by the topic of their conversation whether they want to build relationships or their own ego.

Since narcissists lack empathy, you will often find them struggling with understanding others' perspectives. When someone shares an emotional story or experience, and they might be unable to show the appropriate reaction or say comforting words like you can. That's because they don't understand where others are coming from. Or simply because they don't care. But beware, some narcissists are so good at faking their personalities that they can act like they are empathizing with someone and actually listening to them. Then again, you can tell if their words are genuine or not if you pay close attention to their body language and expressions.

Some people can be too entitled. When you come across a person who thinks they deserve to get whatever they want, even if it's at others' expense, pause and think: Could they be a narcissist?

Time to observe their behavior! If they approach you and you are unable to help them, they will get upset and even say they're disappointed in you. Even when it's not your responsibility to fulfill their demands. They might even try to make you out to be the bad guy! Like you did something wrong when all you did was refuse to help simply because you couldn't. Acting like that really gives the narcissist away.

And they really can't take criticism. So, you can't say anything to them, or they will burst again!

Narcissists are often very materialistic. They believe that having money and possessions equals success and power. These things are more important than actual people and their emotions, so if you see someone who cares more about their riches, that's like they're screaming, "I'm a narcissist."

They will also often talk or act like they are victims. It's because they feel so entitled and perfect that narcissists always feel like others have wronged them. They might talk about past relationships or interactions where they felt mistreated. But if they seem to constantly feel like a victim, it could be a sign of something deeper.

They also love twisting the truth to fit their reality. Narcissists have a way of always wanting to be in control. Sometimes, this means they try to manipulate the truth to fit their own version of events. They may say things like, "Actually, I remember it happening this way," or "I think you're mistaken." While it's important to give others the benefit of the doubt, it's also important to trust your own memories and experiences.

Narcissists have a tendency to keep things to themselves. Their lack of empathy often leads them to act in ways that are less than honest, and they may go so far as to deceive those around them in order to get what they want. They are not forthcoming with information, preferring to share only what is necessary to maintain their carefully crafted image. In short, narcissists are not the most trustworthy individuals, and you should be careful when dealing with them.

Interacting with a self-absorbed narcissist can feel like an uphill battle, especially if you're not sure why they act the way they do. But don't worry; now you know what signs to watch for that can help you protect yourself from their hurtful behavior. While spotting these behaviors won't necessarily guarantee that you'll avoid their manipulation or emotional abuse, it will give you a head start on how to break free from a toxic relationship.

CHAPTER 2:

UNDERSTANDING NARCISSISTIC PERSONALITY DISORDER

While we like to use the term "narcissist" quite casually in recent years, Narcissistic Personality Disorder, or NPD, is actually a formal mental health condition that needs to be diagnosed. It's not just a personality trait or something that someone chooses to have. Understanding this difference is really important if you want to really recognize narcissistic abuse or help someone who's dealing with a narcissist. You see, mental health conditions can have a serious impact on how someone feels, thinks, talks, and behaves in general. And that can affect almost all parts of their life, including their relationships, careers, and daily life in a big way.

People with NPD often have a grandiose sense of self-importance, crave attention and admiration, lack empathy, and have difficulty maintaining relationships. It can be challenging for them to recognize that their behavior is problematic, and most of them do not seek help or treatment on their own. However, with the right support and therapy, individuals with NPD can learn to manage their symptoms and lead fulfilling lives. That is, only if they are willing to seek professional help to get the support needed, which is extremely rare because a narcissist will never admit that they are in the wrong.

27

Scientists have discovered that individuals with NPD may experience challenges in recognizing and comprehending their own thoughts and actions compared to others. Additionally, they might struggle to empathize with the emotions and behaviors of those around them. NPD is classified as a cluster B personality disorder, which is characterized by tendencies toward dramatic, exaggerated, emotional, intense, erratic, and unpredictable behaviors. But here's a lesser-known fact: Most of us display at least one trait that could be considered narcissistic at some point in our lives!

Now, this could be a behavior or attitude that differs from a full-blown personality disorder in terms of how severe, frequent, and longer or shorter it stays. Just like how we all have varying degrees of empathy and generosity, it's the same with narcissistic tendencies. In fact, it's possible that some aspects of narcissism could even be a part of someone's personality. It's all about understanding and navigating these traits and knowing how they differ from someone with NPD.

Sometimes, we may exhibit certain behaviors or thoughts that are related to narcissistic traits but don't necessarily mean we have NPD. For instance, you have a friendly competition with one of your coworkers and you end up making playful jokes or even jokingly bragging about your accomplishments in front of them. However, this is just a momentary reaction. You only did that in a certain situation and with this particular person. It's not a continuous approach or repeated behavior toward anyone else. Nevertheless, in some people, these narcissistic traits can have a permanent impact on their relationships with others and even themselves, causing real harm. It's when a person can't stop but acts that way all the time that we have to suspect NPD.

People who have NPD carry certain repeated, persistent, and distinctive narcissistic traits. For instance, if you know a person who is always struggling and trying to outdo their colleagues, who even believe they are better than their superiors at work, refuses to let go of the delusion that no one else possesses greater intelligence and competence than them, and that they deserve a higher position in the company, this person may have NPD. If this pattern has stayed consistent in their past jobs and even in other areas of their life that only strengthens the suspicion. Now, if you see similar patterns in your personal relationship with them, it's time to be cautious.

Still, remember that only actual professionals can diagnose someone with NPD since it's a serious mental health condition. It's not just about having a high self-esteem or being confident in social situations. These people also carry traits like being extremely competitive, taking too much pride in their accomplishments, and making sure to look their best in terms of their appearance. It's not about them disliking you or anyone, and they are just born that way.

Now, there are many personality disorders out there, and NPD is just one of them. These disorders are types of mental health conditions that are characterized by feelings, thoughts, emotions, and behaviors that can be harmful to the person with the disorder or to those around them. Therefore, these disorders have to be formally diagnosed by mental health professionals. When it comes to NPD, they usually look for two key things, among many other signs, that are:

1. They consider whether a person's personality traits are making it challenging for them to relate to others or even themselves. This might include things like struggles with emotional regulation or difficulty controlling their behavior.
2. Apart from basic personality traits, they look for patterns of these problematic personality traits that crop up in a range of different situations, also called 'pathological personality traits'.

Of course, every person is unique, and this is just a general idea of what might be involved in a personality disorder diagnosis. But when we talk about mental health, "pathological" simply means that a person's thoughts, feelings, or actions are impacting their ability to connect with the world in a positive way.

Sometimes, a physical or mental condition can cause traits that aren't typical or accepted in our society, and this is also considered pathological. Remember that not everyone with a personality disorder experiences the same symptoms or struggles or even the same pathological personality traits, which is why they're broken down into three different categories – more formally known as clusters. In other words, there's a classification system based on personality traits.

Cluster A includes people who are considered "odd or eccentric," while Cluster B is made up of those who tend to be "dramatic and erratic." Cluster C includes individuals who are often "fearful and anxious." And NPD is part of Cluster B!

To diagnose or identify NPD, besides looking for certain patterns, you need to observe at least five of the many specific narcissism symptoms. The Diagnostic and Statistical Manual of Mental Disorders, a handbook used by mental health professionals to accurately diagnose people, has established these NPD symptoms. Before discussing these symptoms, remember that not everyone with a narcissistic personality will experience the same level or intensity of symptoms.

For a diagnosis to be made, at least five of these symptoms need to be present over time and in different situations. While there may not be a clear agreement among experts, some suggest that fragility, fear, and low levels of self-esteem could potentially contribute to certain NPD symptoms.

They believe they are the most important.

Sometimes, people with NPD have a tendency to see themselves as pretty special. They really believe that they are smarter, more intelligent, more clever, more talented, and more any-other-positive-quality than other people. This is why you'll often find them exaggerating their achievements and accomplishments, or even making up lies to look better than others. They sometimes even fake their abilities to feel even more confident about themselves.

Just like how we might try to boost our self-esteem with positive self-talk or compliments, someone with a narcissistic personality does the same by stretching the truth a little bit. But did you know that some people with NPD may not always display a sense of superiority in their behavior? Some narcissists are actually really shy and withdrawn! But they still hold onto the belief that they are superior in certain aspects compared to others.

They often fantasize about being perfect.

We all like to dream big sometimes, but narcissists really take this to a whole another level. Those with NPD have quite the imagination. For example, they may fantasize about having immense power and intelligence, unmatched beauty, or receiving unconditional love and admiration from others. They simply believe they deserve all of this, at least more than others, and they're totally serious about it.

They think they are unique and very special.

Individuals with NPD often have a strong desire to showcase their individuality and distinctiveness when compared to others. This may make them feel more threatened around people and groups with similar unique characteristics. And if someone doesn't understand them because "they're not special enough", the narcissist believes that they are inferior or less intelligent. In a normal person's mind, it would simply mean that they have a different perspective or way of thinking, but those who have NPD just can't help but make everything about themselves.

They need praise and compliments; are attention-seeking.

If a person has NPD, they usually have a strong desire for positive affirmation and recognition. They enjoy being in the spotlight, need constant admiration, and may not handle negative feedback well. Sometimes, they may feel disappointed when others don't share their excitement about their achievements, or if other people think they are not really all that special. Narcissists just don't want to be criticized in any way because they believe they are perfect.

They have a strong sense of entitlement.

A lot of people with NPD believe that they deserve unique consideration and access to all the available benefits. They may also expect everyone else to honor their requests and preferences because they believe they're the only one who matters.

They are manipulative.

It's not uncommon for individuals with narcissistic personality traits to use manipulative and exploitative tactics. Unfortunately, this can mean that they prioritize their personal gain above all else, sometimes taking advantage of others. In some cases, they might even resort to spreading falsehoods about others to further their own goals. They especially do this when their needs are unmet and they want to control the other person to act in a way they want.

They lack empathy.

People with NPD often find it challenging to understand the needs of others or see things from their perspective. This might be why they sometimes behave in ways that are unkind, exploitative, and manipulative. As we have discussed, their lack of empathy can manifest as self-centeredness, disregard for others, and a lack of concern for their feelings.

They feel jealous, don't trust others, and are arrogant.

It's common for people with NPD to think that others are trying to outdo them. This is why they feel jealous of others' successes. Similarly, they may find themselves constantly striving to keep up with others or feeling a twinge of jealousy toward their achievements. These people simply struggle to see the value in others. This mindset often leads them to act in overconfident or dismissive ways, as they believe they are the only ones deserving of respect and kindness.

Narcissism vs. NPD

Did you know that Narcissistic Personality Disorder is one of the least explored personality disorders? Because of this, it can be challenging to comprehend its root causes and potential treatment options. There is currently very little consensus within the medical community about what triggers the development of NPD. However, many experts believe that environmental and cultural influences, early life experiences, and genetics may all play a role.

Simply put, a person may have developed traits of narcissism due to certain experiences they faced from a very young age. These could include going through a traumatic event as a child, feeling neglected or abandoned by their guardian, receiving a lot of negative remarks, growing up with a parent or guardian who has a mental illness, being subjected to some kind of abuse, and facing discrimination. Similarly, being excessively pampered and spoiled as a child can also contribute to this. And, of course, having a family history of NPD also increases their chances of developing the same condition.

It's important to remember that everyone's experiences and circumstances are unique, and it's understandable that some may develop coping mechanisms that may seem like narcissistic behavior. This does not mean they have NPD. We all react differently to certain events, making it tricky to recognize a narcissist from a normal person. Still, as we learned, there are certain patterns and pathological traits that we can look out for. Even researchers find it hard to pinpoint the exact causes of personality disorders!

In other words, not every narcissist has NPD. It's understandable for you to be curious about the narcissists in your life and wonder if they have NPD, but it's best to leave the diagnosis

35

to a professional. Remember that NPD is a complex condition that can't just be diagnosed based on a few observations or behaviors. And while it might be tempting to try and diagnose someone you know, it's really best to leave the diagnosis up to trained mental health professionals like psychiatrists or psychologists. These experts have the knowledge and experience to diagnose properly after thoroughly evaluating the person and their medical history.

And you know that? Only up to 5% of people are suspected to have NPD. We can't really have an exact number of people with NPD because the diagnosis depends on many factors, such as their willingness to seek treatment. Unfortunately, many people with this disorder do not seek help. After all, why would they think anything is wrong with them? What's even more interesting is that NPD diagnoses are more common among men, with 50 to 75% of those diagnosed being male. That doesn't mean women can't be narcissists! It just means men are more often seen exhibiting these traits than women.

So, if you're concerned about someone's behavior or mental health, it's always a good idea to encourage them to seek help from a qualified professional.

It's not always a walk in the park for mental health professionals to diagnose NPD, even with all their expertise. The challenge arises from the fact that people with NPD are less likely to seek help, share their innermost thoughts, or attend therapy sessions. In any case, mental health experts use the DSM-5 framework to diagnose NPD.

They take a closer look at several aspects of a person's life, including their unique personality traits, how they function in the world, how they form and maintain relationships, and may even take a look at their job history. It's also important to look into their sense of identity, self-esteem, and any changes in how they view themselves over time. And, of course, the health professional will determine if the person displays empathy.

When seeking help for NPD, a mental health professional will typically look for five or more symptoms to make a diagnosis and recommend treatment. While some teenagers may exhibit early signs of the disorder, it's typically diagnosed in adulthood due to ongoing physical and mental development during adolescence. It can be challenging to identify lasting patterns of behavior in young people due to these ongoing changes.

What Therapists Say About NPD

According to Dr Ramani Durvasula, a licensed clinical psychologist, narcissistic personality disorder is often misunderstood. Many people see NPD as a condition characterized by excessive self-esteem and arrogance. While these traits are indeed part of it, narcissism actually stems from low self-esteem. "People with narcissism are often the most insecure people in the room," she says. "And they've established a way of showing themselves as anything but."

Narcissists have developed a skill for portraying themselves as confident when there is a void inside them in reality! She also mentions that four key elements can characterize narcissism:

1. A limited capacity for understanding others' feelings
2. An inclination toward exaggerated self-importance
3. An ongoing belief in deserving special treatment
4. An incessant desire for admiration and validation from those around them.

These factors essentially form the foundation of this disorder.

Dr Brenda Wade, another clinical psychologist says that people with NPD will always make you feel like you're the one at fault, in the wrong, and the problem. In her words,

"Narcissists:

- Think of themselves first and foremost.
- Only want to win.
- Do not care about your feelings.
- Are always manipulating for their own personal gain and benefit.
- Make you think that you are the problem.
- Gaslighting is their stock and trade."

According to most psychologists who work with patients, it is commonly believed that both grandiosity and vulnerability can exist within the same person, manifesting in different situations.

However, there is a debate within the academic community as some experts argue that these traits do not always coexist. And this discussion is yet to reach a conclusion even after years because people with NPD will rarely ever willingly go for treatment and show vulnerability in front of someone.

According to Elsa Ronningstam, a clinical psychologist, there are different types of narcissism. The first one, which is relatively functional, involves having a positive self-image and a genuine desire to take care of oneself. People with this kind of narcissism are also capable of maintaining close relationships with others and accepting differences between themselves and their idealized selves. On the other hand, there is another type called "pathological" narcissism, where individuals struggle to maintain a stable sense of self-worth.

These individuals protect an exaggerated view of themselves, disregarding the feelings of others. When their inflated self-image is threatened, they might experience negative emotions like anger, shame, or envy. It's important to note that these individuals can lead mostly normal lives, only acting out in specific situations.

Narcissistic personality disorder is a subset of pathological narcissism, characterized by long-term and persistent issues. It often coexists with other conditions such as depression, bipolar disorder, borderline personality disorder, or antisocial personality disorder.

Remember, narcissists exist on a spectrum, and those with NPD are at the highest end. If you suspect someone you know to have this disorder and you've been subjected to narcissistic abuse, seeking help is always a positive step toward better mental health!

CHAPTER 3:

THE MOMENT YOU REALIZE

It can be tough to accept, but the truth is that the person who ended up being a narcissist probably never truly loved you, not even at the start. It can be challenging to navigate your emotions and logic in this situation.

Have you ever found it difficult to remember your worth when your heart is involved? It's like our emotions have a way of clouding our judgment, even when we know we deserve better. We end up tolerating things we shouldn't just because of our attachment to someone. Wouldn't it be nice if there was a magic switch we could flip to turn off those emotions and make walking away less painful? Let's remember our worth and make sure we're treating ourselves with love and respect.

Discovering that someone you care about is a narcissist can be a challenging first step. It's a step that requires strength and courage. Although it's not always easy, acknowledging this can be an empowering and liberating experience. It's okay to feel hurt and confused, as this realization can impact your self-esteem and relationships. However, it also presents an opportunity for growth and self-discovery. By recognizing and understanding your

41

emotions, you can take control of your life and create positive changes. Remember, you're not alone in this journey, and there's always support available to guide you along the way.

When you realize the person you've loved and cared for so much never actually felt the same way about you, it's normal to feel like you've lost everything. You might feel that you've lost you:

Self-esteem

Have you ever been in a situation where you've put so much effort into a relationship or friendship, but it seems the other person doesn't appreciate it? It can really take a toll on our self-esteem and make us question ourselves and our abilities to build meaningful connections. But let me tell you, it's not your fault! Don't beat yourself up over it. Your self-worth is not determined by someone else's inability to recognize your value. Remember to always prioritize your own happiness and well-being.

Social life

It's completely understandable that discovering that someone close to us is a narcissist can cause some turbulence in our relationships. It may affect our social circle and even our direct connection with the individual. However, it's important to approach the situation with empathy and compassion. Confronting a narcissist about their behavior can lead to an explosive reaction, so it's best to tread carefully. It's also important to remember that not everyone may view the situation in the same light as you do. But with patience and understanding, we can navigate through this tough time and come out stronger on the other side.

Plans

Things can take a turn for the worse when we finally see that the person we've been supporting is a narcissist. It's a total game-changer. Once you realize your loved one has some narcissistic tendencies, your plans might have to be put on hold for a bit. It could throw a wrench in your wedding plans or cause some turmoil in your family dynamic. But don't worry, this realization can also bring about a much-needed shift in perspective. It's all about waking up to who someone truly is and moving forward with that newfound knowledge.

Self

Did you ever experience a difficult phase in your life while trying to build a future with a narcissist? Unfortunately, there is a sad reality that many of them tend to manipulate and gaslight us in a way that makes us feel disconnected from our true selves. It's like suddenly waking up to their deceit and realizing that everything you thought was real was just an illusion. It can leave you feeling lost and confused, and the person you once knew seems like a stranger. This can have a significant impact on your self-esteem and relationships, but it's important to remember that you're not alone. There's always a way to heal and rediscover your worth.

Have you ever found yourself being really resourceful in tough situations? It's actually quite common for people who have experienced narcissistic abuse to develop this skill. When we're not given the attention, affection, and support we need, we learn to rely on ourselves. While this can be a great thing, it's important to be aware that it can also be harmful. Sometimes, we can become so independent that we shut others out and feel alone. Remember, it's okay to ask for help and let others in. You don't have to handle everything on your own.

The Hardest Reality

Navigating through narcissistic abuse can be really tough, but one of the biggest challenges is accepting the truth. It's important to acknowledge your reality for what it is rather than how the narcissist wants you to see it or how you wish it to be. It can be hard to accept that the person you care about isn't the same person you truly need or want them to be. The narcissist will never be the person you thought they were - their facade was always just that, a facade. But don't worry; you're not alone in this, and there's always hope for healing and moving forward.

Let's face it: sometimes people can be a little deceptive. Narcissists, in particular, tend to get caught up in their own stories and end up deceiving not only themselves but others, too. But no matter how skilled they are at spinning their tales, the truth will always come out in the end. It's really tough when you realize that your relationship with a narcissist wasn't what you thought it was.

You had hoped for the best, but it turns out that everything was a lie. But don't worry, and you're not alone. It happens to the best of us.

Now, it's time to move forward and see things for what they really are. Instead of focusing on what you thought it was or what you wanted it to be, embrace the reality of the situation and use it as a learning experience.

Let's take a moment to reflect on what's really going on. What do you see in your current situation? What do you know to be true? It's important to acknowledge that trusting a narcissist can lead to misery and disappointment. But don't worry, we're here to support you and help you see things clearly. Take a step back and see the situation for what it is. It may be tough, but it's important not to sugarcoat it.

Remember, the narcissist may be causing harm, but you have the power to take control of your life and move forward. Stay strong and don't let them destroy you.

It can be really, really hard to end a toxic relationship, especially when you've been through psychological abuse and manipulation. Sometimes, you even feel like you're stuck in a fantasy world and can't imagine leaving. But there's often more to the story than you realize - maybe you're working through past trauma or trying to heal wounds from your families. Regardless, it's important to remember that you have the power to break free and find healthier relationships.

You know what they say – looks can be deceiving! Especially when it comes to toxic relationships. That's why it's important to take a step back and seek support from trusted friends or professionals. Sometimes, we're so caught up in the midst of it all that we can't see the bigger picture. By taking a breather and looking at things from a different perspective, we can better understand what's really going on.

Sometimes, we find ourselves in a difficult spot because we care deeply for our narcissistic loved ones. We hold on tight to their stories as if our happiness depended on it. Before we know it, we're entwined with them, letting go of our independence and handing over the reins of our mental and emotional state. Unfortunately, we're living a lie just like they are.

It's easy to feel overwhelmed when you're dealing with a narcissist. Their disordered reality can seep into your own, leaving you feeling confused and lost. Unfortunately, this confusion can take its toll, and some victims may even experience a breaking point. But don't lose hope, and healing is possible once you break free from the cycle of abuse.

Whether you decide to stay with your narcissistic partner until they leave you or take the brave step of cutting ties and focusing on your own worth and healing, know that the road ahead may be long and difficult. But don't let that discourage you! No matter what, taking care of yourself and getting out of a toxic situation is always the better option. So, be kind to yourself, and remember that you can and will overcome this.

Another thing to remember: narcissists work in a parasitic way - they're always seeking a host, and it's definitely not love that they're after. But don't beat yourself up about it, because no matter what you did, the outcome wouldn't have changed. It might take some time and commitment, but taking care of yourself and removing the parasite from your life is so worth it. You deserve to have a life free from the negative effects of their behavior, and you can do it! Remember to choose yourself and reality over the narcissist's twisted role-play.

You are worth so much, and it's time to take your power back. So keep your head up, own your worth, and know that you can overcome this.

Narcissist Breakup vs. Regular Breakup

A healthy, normal relationship is one where you can support each other and help each other through tough times. It's not about finding someone to control your emotions but rather someone who can help you navigate them. When these basic things are not present in the relationship, it can't be healthy. Whether it's just a friend or a partner, you need to be a team, face challenges together, and hold hands as you take each step with genuine curiosity and understanding.

Healthy relationships are all about being there for each other without judgment or bad intentions and helping each other grow. It's based on trust and support. They're here for you, and you're here for them. But sometimes, things just don't work out, and you drift apart. That's normal, too.

Breakups can be hard, but with time comes an opportunity to reflect on the lessons we learned from past relationships. It's possible that the person you once loved will continue to hold a special place in your heart. However, when it comes to relationships with narcissists, things can be quite different.

So, what exactly defines a narcissistic breakup, and why does it feel so challenging and harder than a regular one?

People who exhibit narcissistic traits tend to have an avoidant attachment style. This means they aren't very affectionate and intimate, at least not genuinely. Instead, they manipulate and gaslight you into thinking that they do. Most narcissists grow up lacking parental affection or love from a guardian, which explains their tendency to be avoidant and cold. However, it's important to know that not all narcissists fit the stereotypical images of them.

Some people believe that narcissists only love material things like money and looks. That's true because grandiose narcissists are the ones who tend to care about these things. But on the other hand, covert or vulnerable narcissists are a bit different. They too have grandiose fantasies but feel inadequate, are often introverted, and struggle with anxiety and emptiness.

What makes breaking up with a narcissist so different from a typical breakup? It all comes down to one thing: It's what you are made to believe. When you first enter into a relationship with a narcissist, they will use all sorts of love-bombing tactics to keep you hooked because they know you are a great source of validation for them. As a result, their brains become flooded with feel-good hormones like dopamine and oxytocin, which can make their love for you feel incredibly intense.

Individuals with narcissistic tendencies have a different perception of love compared to those who are emotionally mature and well-adjusted. To them, love is merely viewed as a transaction, even when they are experiencing the intense rush of love hormones that they become addicted to. They might express a keen interest in your dreams and aspirations, and may even offer to provide you with the life you deserve, but know that none of that is genuine.

Additionally, narcissists also try to gain access to your private information in order to manipulate you later on. This is often followed by a gradual process of devaluation and eventually discarding you altogether. They might even mirror your behavior to make you trust them more. While mirroring is okay at times, doing so without any real intention of building a genuine connection is not okay.

Don't ever take a narcissist's words to heart. They are more focused on chasing a fantasy fairytale than finding a real relationship or person. When you try to engage with them or offer them helpful advice, they will not reciprocate and even dismiss you entirely. That's all because, deep down, they are not ready to confront their own emotions.

As you journey through your relationship, there will come a point where you feel devalued and ultimately discarded. It can be a tough pill to swallow, and you may feel blindsided by it all. The emotions that flood in can be overwhelming – from pain to anger and a sense of loss for not just the relationship but for the person you thought you knew.

After the discard, you may wonder what happens next. Will they move on quickly to a new person to trap, leaving you feeling completely devastated? But remember, they never truly had a deep connection with you. They may be searching for someone new to fill their inner void because they can't face it alone. You should know that you deserve someone who values and appreciates you for who you are.

Perhaps the most challenging obstacle to overcome is the deliberate manipulation and emotional turmoil inflicted by the narcissist. These individuals tend to harbor anger and misery and often project these negative emotions onto those closest to them. As the initial bliss of a relationship fades, you may struggle to comprehend why your partner is pulling away or treating you poorly. You may question your own actions and feel ignored or confused.

Dealing with a narcissist's unpredictable behavior can be emotionally draining. Their tendency to give mixed signals – expressing affection one day and disdain the next – can leave you feeling confused and questioning your own worth. Unfortunately, narcissists are notorious for their dishonesty, even about the smallest things. If caught in a lie, they will try to deflect blame or become irrationally angry.

If you decide to end the relationship, the narcissist may feel hurt and vulnerable. This is because they believe they are special, superior, and unique, and any perceived slight can be difficult for them to handle. They will feel angry or sad about the breakup, but it's not because they are not mourning the loss of a loved one, but rather the damage to their ego and the effort they put into securing that supply.

Although their grieving process may not be very long, they also won't typically take responsibility for their actions. As a result, the breakup may not resonate with them in the way that you expect. They will eventually let go by telling themselves that you're simply crazy or that they're better off without you. This is a part of their devaluation process, but please know that it doesn't diminish the amount of time or suffering that you may have experienced. Don't let the opinions of others dictate your self-worth.

With a regular breakup, you grieve the loss and finally move on. But narcissists will cling to you just because they can't lose their "supply" that they get from you. They never loved you. But in a regular relationship, you might have loved each other genuinely. In most cases, when a regular relationship ends, both individuals tend to part ways and move forward. However, when dealing with a narcissist, things can be quite tricky. The relationship may end suddenly without any warning, or it may never end at all.

Narcissists tend to be very controlling and like to keep a hold on their partners, even after the breakup. They often offer staying friends after a breakup if they were your partner or ask to keep in touch as a means of maintaining a connection. That, again, is also only for their own supply. They want to continue receiving your attention, affection, and even resources without commitment. Unfortunately, this can prevent you from moving on.

Narcissists can be really clever. It's amazing how they can effortlessly pick up on when you start moving on from them. And then, suddenly, they reappear in your life, showering you with affection like nothing ever happened. You might think to yourself, "Wow, maybe they finally realized how great I am and things will be different this time!" But don't be too quick to jump to conclusions. Just remember that this person has a history of putting on an act, and it won't be long before their true colors show once again. So, if they come back into your life, don't be swayed and keep your emotions in check. Never, ever invite them back into your life.

It's true that some people have the ability to manipulate others without a second thought. But guess what? You have that same power at your fingertips. Your mind is the captain of your ship, so make sure you're always aware of what's going on up there, especially when you're feeling emotional. If you can keep your emotions in check and let your mind drive, you'll be in a super strong position.

Embracing change can be beautiful, especially in relationships with those who may exhibit narcissistic tendencies. If you've experienced narcissistic abuse, it's natural to reach a point where you recognize the need for a shift. Maybe you've realized that one more negative interaction could have serious consequences, or perhaps you've noticed that you're not progressing as you should be. When we're pushed to the edge, we're given the opportunity to see things more clearly and make positive changes. Remember, change is a chance to grow and move forward.

CHAPTER 4:

TYPES OF NARCISSISM

We now know how narcissism and NPD differ from each other and that a person having narcissistic tendencies may not necessarily be a narcissist. But did you know that while someone can receive a diagnosis of narcissistic personality disorder, there isn't any official clinical diagnosis for different subtypes of narcissism? It's true! Although some types of narcissism have been backed up by research from other professionals, other types have been given informal names by mental health experts. So, it's difficult to put a specific number on the amount of narcissistic subtypes out there.

At the end of the day, you must remember that narcissism is just a trait that falls on a spectrum of human behavior.

Here are some of the common types of narcissists:

Overt

Overt narcissists, also called grandiose narcissists, have an unrealistic sense of superiority. These people overestimate their abilities and constantly assert dominance over others. They also tend to have an inflated sense of self-esteem. This type of narcissism has also been studied and confirmed by researchers, so you know it exist!

People with grandiose narcissism openly exhibit qualities like entitlement, bragging, and excessive self-absorption. Unfortunately, this often comes at the expense of others. While these individuals can be charming, they often lack empathy and don't relate well to others. You might notice that they constantly try to one-up people in conversations, seeking attention and even enjoying seeing others hurt or confused.

If you find yourself interacting with an overt narcissist, or any other type of narcissist for that matter, it's important to set boundaries. Remember, these individuals will push your limits and try to wear down your boundaries until how they treat you becomes the new normal. So, be prepared to enforce those boundaries, and don't be afraid to walk away if necessary. It's all about taking care of yourself and not letting anyone treat you poorly.

Covert

This type of narcissist, called covert narcissist, is also known as a vulnerable narcissist. Unlike overt narcissists who are confident and showy, these people tend to be on the shy and self-effacing side. According to the American Journal of Psychiatry (AJP), the "covert subtype is inhibited, manifestly distressed, hypersensitive to the evaluations of others while chronically envious." They really want to be recognized and appreciated by others, and criticism can make them feel defensive.

It's important to remember that covert narcissists can struggle with feelings of misery and often believe that their suffering is worse than anyone else's. While it's understandable that they may have been hurt in the past, it's not your job to save or look out for them. Remember that setting boundaries is also important for your own well-being!

Malignant

As the name suggests, people with malignant narcissism tend to manipulate and harm others. They may exhibit signs of sadistic behavior and aggression. According to the American Journal of Psychiatry, they are considered the most severe type of narcissistic personality disorder. It's true that they're quite different from your typical narcissist because they also have an antisocial personality disorder, which can make things even more challenging. They can never empathize with others and can be quite ruthless.

We already know that narcissists lack empathy, but when it comes to malignant narcissists, their actions are downright hurtful. Causing other people pain gives them a sense of authority and gratification. It's not uncommon for them to take pleasure in knowing they have the ability to harm others. And this seems to be a favorite pastime of theirs. Malignant narcissists are also more upfront about their intentions and less sneaky than other narcissistic types. They often resort to tactics like threatening their victims to get what they want.

It's crucial that you steer clear of these individuals and sever all ties if you know one. Trying to outsmart them can be both exhausting and fruitless. They have spent a lot of time honing their skills in becoming better at narcissism, and they may even take pleasure in seeing others feel pain and discomfort. Remember to prioritize your own well-being and surround yourself with positive, supportive people. Don't ever let a malignant narcissist suck your energy away!

Antagonistic

Antagonistic narcissism is often said to be a subtype of overt narcissism. These types of narcissists are mostly focused on competing. They tend to exhibit manipulative and aggressive behaviors, and may sometimes rely on others to achieve their goals. Antagonistic narcissists also take advantage of people for their own benefit. They are highly competitive and enjoy being in the spotlight. However, such behavior can have damaging consequences for themselves and those around them.

Some behaviors are commonly associated with antagonistic narcissism, like always criticizing and putting others down, demanding excessive attention and compliance, resorting to threats or even physical violence, and manipulating and exploiting others for personal gain. People with antagonistic narcissism often cause emotional or physical harm to others and use their power or position to disrupt their lives. They have a harder time forgiving others than those with other types of narcissism, and they may also have lower trust in others.

It can be tough to break free if you find yourself in a relationship with someone who displays these traits. But it's important to remember that you are not responsible for their actions. Don't hesitate to reach out to loved ones or a trained professional if you need help getting out of the situation. Remember, you're never alone!

Communal

Communal narcissism is also a type of overt narcissism but is often viewed as the opposite of antagonistic narcissism. People with communal narcissism tend to place a high value on fairness and consider themselves altruistic. However, there can sometimes be a disconnect between their beliefs and their actual behavior. These individuals may seem morally outraged quite easily and often describe themselves as generous and empathetic. They are also known to react strongly when they perceive something as unfair.

You might be wondering how communal narcissism differs from genuine concern for others' well-being. The answer lies in the fact that communal narcissists tend to prioritize social power and self-importance. Although they may claim to have a strong moral code and care for others, their actions may not necessarily align with their words. It's important to be self-aware and make sure our treatment of others matches up with our beliefs, and if you come across a communal narcissist, you know what to do!

Spiritual

Some people may use their spirituality in a negative way, such as to justify harmful behaviors or make others feel intimidated. And if they display narcissistic tendencies too, well, we've got a spiritual narcissist! Keep in mind that their behavior stems from a need to present a perfect image to escape personal insecurities. Unfortunately, those going through a difficult time or experiencing a big change may be more susceptible to these narcissists' influence.

If you find yourself in a situation where someone is using their spirituality to manipulate or belittle you, it's okay to take a step back and separate yourself from that person. Remember that true spirituality is about kindness, compassion, and understanding; those who use it negatively do not embody those values. Stay strong and surround yourself with positivity!

Sexual

Have you ever met someone who was just overly confident in their bedroom abilities? Well, these people are called sexual narcissists! They tend to have an inflated ego regarding their sexual prowess and crave the admiration of others. Unfortunately, this can lead to some pretty toxic behaviors like cheating, using sex as a means of manipulation, and even violent behavior.

If you find yourself in a relationship with a sexual narcissist, it's important to prioritize your own well-being and consider seeking therapy to help you navigate the breakup. Remember, healthy relationships include being with someone who values and respects you in all aspects of your relationship - not just in the bedroom.

Sexual narcissism is one of the three different types of narcissism, including somatic and cerebral narcissism. While there isn't much research to support this typing system, some mental health practitioners are finding it helpful in better understanding and categorizing different types of narcissism. Remember that there are various ways narcissism can manifest itself!

Somatic

Have you ever met someone who just can't stop talking about how amazing their body is? Well, that's what we call a somatic narcissist. They derive their self-worth from their physical appearance, which can sometimes lead to them feeling superior to others. It's common for them to obsess over their weight and appearance; unfortunately, this often leads to them criticizing others based on their looks.

If you're dealing with a somatic narcissist, staying calm and not reacting emotionally to their behavior is best. Trust me, they thrive on drama!

Cerebral

Have you ever met someone who seems to take all their self-worth from their intellect? These are what we call cerebral narcissists. They may not be as obvious as the somatic kind who derive their worth from their appearance, but cerebral narcissists still have an insatiable need to feel smarter, more clever, and more intelligent than others.

Dealing with a cerebral narcissist can be hard, especially if they're always trying to make you feel inferior. So, here's a friendly piece of advice: Instead of getting caught up in their arguments, try not to take their words to heart. Remember, you don't have to prove yourself to them or anyone else. Just focus on being the best version of yourself and let them be.

CHAPTER 5:

SIGNS AND SYMPTOMS OF NARCISSISTIC ABUSE

Picture this: your world has undergone a transformation, but not a good one. You've been treated unfairly, deceived, and made to feel like you're imagining things. The person you once knew and the life you shared have been broken into tiny pieces. You feel like you've lost touch with who you are and your worth has been belittled. You were put on a pedestal, then taken down and pushed away. Maybe this happened multiple times, and you were even replaced, but somehow, you were convinced to come back to a relationship that was even more painful than before. Perhaps you were followed, bothered, and made to feel uncomfortable just to keep you tied to your abuser.

Sometimes, breakups can be tough but some are even worse. Unfortunately, some people can use a breakup as a way to harm you emotionally and make you feel unsafe in the world. And the worst part is that you might not even see any physical scars. Instead, you feel like you have a bunch of scattered memories and emotional wounds. This type of situation is called narcissistic abuse, and it's definitely not okay.

At the heart of narcissism lies an excessive focus on oneself, often leading to entitlement and selfishness. Unfortunately, some people with narcissistic traits take this to the extreme, displaying a superiority complex and a lack of empathy toward others. Dealing with a partner or a loved one with such tendencies can be challenging, especially considering their manipulative behaviors. It's not uncommon for those in relationships with narcissists to take months or even years to recognize the abuse they're experiencing. The good news is that with the right support and resources, it's possible to heal and move forward.

The first step is understanding and recognizing what's happening or has happened to you. Narcissistic abuse is a really harmful behavior where someone in a relationship humiliates and blames their partner, essentially destroying them. It's definitely not love, and unfortunately, narcissists tend to feed off their victim's attention and powerlessness. It's almost like they need someone to constantly stroke their ego and make them feel important. The scary part is that narcissists can often be incredibly charming at first, so it's not always easy to spot the warning signs. Just remember, you deserve a healthy, respectful relationship.

Here are 10 signs to look out for if you suspect you're currently in a relationship with a narcissist:

1. Your relationship was intense in the early stages

If you've found yourself in a relationship that started with a bang, you might want to look closer. Narcissists can be incredibly charming and make you feel like you've found your soulmate right away. They'll pour on the love and affection, making you feel like you're on top of the world. But be wary if things feel a bit too intense too soon, and there's never a moment of peace. Remember, healthy relationships are built on trust, respect, and a healthy dose of calm.

2. It's quickly losing its spark

Another thing to remember is that sometimes the initial spark with a narcissist can fade. Instead of feeling like you're their perfect match, they might start making you doubt yourself and feel like you're not good enough. Never listen to them! There are plenty of amazing people out there who will appreciate and value you for who you are.

3. It seems like they're no longer interested

Another sign that things may be changing in your relationship is when you start to feel like your partner isn't fully engaged in your conversations. At first, it may have felt like they were hanging onto every word, but as time goes on, you might start to feel like you're not being heard. This is one of the many tactics narcissists use against their victims. Their goal was always to trap you, so they had to act charming in the beginning before they started to show their true colors.

It's true that this issue can also arise in a healthy relationship, but you can address it with your partner in that case since you would have open communication. A narcissist will instead blame you or disregard your concerns.

4. They are no longer nice to you

One thing to keep in mind is that some people might not have the best intentions when they communicate with you. It's on you to recognize when someone says things that hurt your feelings or make you doubt yourself. A narcissist, for example, might comment on your clothing choices or suggest that you aren't capable of achieving your dreams. They love to be mean for no reason just to feel good about themselves, so remember it's all lies.

It's always good to surround yourself with positive and encouraging people who lift you up and make you feel good about yourself. It's all about communication. When you encounter someone who speaks in a hurtful manner, it can really take a toll on your self-esteem. So, remember that some people may intentionally try to bring you down, but that doesn't mean their words hold any truth! Remember that you are smart, you are worthy, and you are beautiful inside and out.

5. Gaslighting

Another crucial thing to keep an eye out for is when someone tries to make you doubt your own perception of reality. This can happen when a person says something to you but denies ever saying it when you repeat it. This can be very confusing and leave you feeling unsure of yourself. This would be a common occurrence if you're in a relationship with a narcissist. So, remember, you are capable of knowing what's happening in your life, and don't let anyone make you think otherwise!

6. They always blame you

One way to recognize a healthy relationship is when both parties feel comfortable expressing themselves without fear of blame. On the other hand, in most cases, people who are in a relationship with a narcissist may hesitate to speak their minds. This is because they could be blamed for anything, even things that are not their fault. It's vital to understand that this is not a reflection of you, and you are not responsible for every negative thing that happens in the relationship. Don't ever listen to a narcissist or accept the blame that is put on you. Always remember that healthy relationships are built on trust and mutual respect.

7. You feel less and less confident

Have you ever noticed that sometimes you second-guess your decisions? Maybe it's just a moment of uncertainty, but if it's happening more frequently, it could be a sign that you're with a narcissist. Over time, the constant belittling and criticism from a narcissistic person can cause you to lose faith in your own decision-making abilities. This can lead to feelings of uncertainty and hesitation when faced with choices and can ultimately harm your self-esteem.

Trusting yourself is so important, and sometimes, when we're around people who don't support us, it can be tough to maintain that confidence. Remember that your skills and talents are valuable, no matter what others say!

8. Depression and anxiety

It's important to take note of how you're feeling, and if you've been struggling with depression and anxiety lately, it's possible that you might be experiencing the effects of narcissistic abuse. You might constantly feel on edge and worried about when the next hurtful comment or action will come your way. It's understandable to want to make others happy, but it's important to remember to care for yourself too. If you're feeling unappreciated and drained from constantly putting others before yourself, it might be time to reevaluate the situation and prioritize your own well-being.

9. You don't feel like yourself

Another signal that could indicate that you have been in a relationship with a narcissistic partner for a while is that you may no longer feel like yourself. This could be because you have been bending over backward to fit your partner's every whim and desire, hoping to keep them happy. This kind of constant accommodation can lead to losing touch with your own identity, making it hard to recognize yourself. It's important to remember that you can and should seek help if you feel like you have lost touch with who that person is.

Sometimes when we are in such a situation, we may find ourselves changing who we are to try and please the narcissist. This could mean doing things we don't necessarily enjoy because we're afraid of upsetting them. It can also make it hard to know what we truly believe in and want for ourselves. Remember that it's okay to be yourself and prioritize your own happiness and needs.

10. Isolation

A warning sign to watch out for in a relationship is if you find yourself spending less and less time with your friends and family. Your partner or friend may not necessarily be abusive, but it's important to recognize when you're being pulled away from those who care about you. It's natural to want to spend time with the person you're in a relationship with, but if it comes at the cost of your other relationships, it's worth taking a step back and evaluating whether this is a healthy dynamic. Sometimes, it can be easy to get caught up in a new relationship and lose touch with people you used to be close to, but if you're isolating yourself out of fear or pressure from your partner, it's a red flag. Trust your instincts and don't let anyone control who you can or can't spend time with.

Now, let's get a bit more specific and talk about the journey of a victim of narcissistic abuse.

Malignant narcissists are the most abusive type since they use harmful behavior to manipulate and control others. Their actions can range from hurtful language and emotional manipulation to more complex tactics like spreading rumors and ignoring communication. Remember that these behaviors can only be carried out by those who lack empathy and prioritize their own needs over the well-being of others. When you experience chronic abuse from them, it can really take a toll on your mental health.

Some victims even experience symptoms of PTSD or Complex PTSD, especially if they've been through multiple traumatic experiences, such as being abused by narcissistic parents or developing Narcissistic Victim Syndrome. This can lead to a whole host of issues like depression, anxiety, feeling on edge all the time, an overwhelming sense of shame, and even flashbacks that transport the victim back to those painful experiences.

It can be tough to recognize the signs of abuse when you're in the middle of it. Abusers have a way of manipulating reality to fit their needs, making it hard to identify what's happening. They might even show you love and affection after hurting you, making you think that you're the one in the wrong.

If you can answer yes to most of the questions below and you're in a relationship with someone who disrespects and mistreats you, there's a high chance that you've been dealing with emotional and narcissistic abuse:

Do you feel detached from yourself and everything around you?

Have you ever felt like you're not really present in the moment? Like your mind is elsewhere, and you're not really sure what's going on around you? That's called dissociation, and it's actually a natural survival mechanism. When we experience trauma or overwhelming emotions, our brain can shut down and detach from the situation to protect us. It can feel strange and unsettling, but it's actually a way for our minds to cope.

Sometimes, our brains simply shut down our emotions. This can make it hard to feel anything at all, and we might find ourselves doing things that distract us from our problems. Whether watching a lot of TV, playing video games, or getting into a hobby, these activities can help us feel like we're in a different world where we don't have to deal with our problems.

Are you always walking on eggshells around your partner/abuser?

Have you ever found yourself feeling a bit apprehensive around a certain person in your life? Sometimes past experiences can cause us to avoid anything that reminds us of those difficult times. This may mean being cautious around certain individuals, like friends, family members, colleagues, or bosses. You might catch yourself carefully choosing your words or actions just to avoid any potential conflict or negative reactions.

If you have ever tried to brush off your abuser's hurtful behavior only to find that it doesn't seem to make a difference, well - that's another red flag. It can be frustrating and disheartening to feel like you're constantly being targeted as their emotional punching bag. You may even start to feel anxious about accidentally provoking them, which can make it difficult to stand up for yourself or set boundaries. Unfortunately, this can bleed into other areas of your life, leading to people-pleasing behavior and a loss of self-confidence. Remember, you deserve to be treated with kindness and respect!

Do you feel physically weak or sick?

Living with a narcissist can make you go through tough health issues and experience physical symptoms that might be linked to emotional struggles. Maybe you've noticed some changes in your weight or have developed new health concerns causing you to worry. Chronic abuse can really take a toll on your body, impacting your stress levels and immune system. This can leave you feeling vulnerable and struggling to get restful sleep. If you're experiencing flashbacks or nightmares related to past traumas, know that you're not alone. Remember to take care of yourself, both physically and emotionally.

Do you often mistrust others?

It can become a habit to keep your guard up after experiencing the malicious actions of someone you once trusted. You might find yourself feeling anxious about the intentions of others and be extra cautious. However, it's important to remember that not everyone is out to get you. Even though your experiences may have been invalidated in the past, it's key to trust yourself and others who have earned your trust. Remember, many wonderful people in the world will treat you with much more respect and genuineness!

Do you feel forced to give up on your goals and dreams?

Have you ever felt hesitant to pursue your passions and achieve your goals? Unfortunately, some individuals who suffer from narcissistic abuse may experience this fear. These predators are so envious of their victims that they use punishment as a means of control. Over time, you may begin to associate your talents and successes with negative treatment. And as a result, you may develop a fear of success and worry about facing criticism or retaliation. You might also start to feel down and worried and lose your self-assurance.

Unfortunately, all of this can lead you to shy away from the spotlight and let your abuser take center stage time and time again. But it's important to remember that your abuser isn't trying to bring you down because they think you're not good enough. It's just that your amazing talents and abilities threaten their hold over you. So keep shining bright because you are truly amazing!

Are you neglecting your needs?

Initially, you may have been a person full of vitality and dreams with a clear sense of purpose. However, when in a relationship with an abuser, many victims often neglect their needs and desires just to satisfy their abusers. Your emotional and physical well-being might have been compromised in the same way. At times, it can feel like your entire life revolves around the abuser, leaving little room for your own hobbies, friendships, me-time, and safety. It's important to remember that no matter how much you try to please them, it will never be enough. Remember, your own happiness and well-being are just as important!

Do you often compare yourself to others?

Living with a narcissist can make you feel like you're just not good enough. These abusers often bring other people into the relationship to create drama and make their victims feel inadequate. Hence, it's common for victims to question their worth and wonder why they're being treated so poorly.

Sometimes, you might even find yourself comparing your situation to others who seem to be in happier and healthier relationships. It's natural to wonder why your abuser is treating complete strangers with more respect. It's normal to have feelings of self-blame, or even question "why me?" But let's get one thing straight – you are not to blame for the abuse you have suffered. The responsibility lies solely with the abuser. Never let the abuser's manipulation and mind games make you doubt yourself. You are enough just the way you are.

If you're currently in a situation where you're being mistreated or abused, just know that you're not alone. Even if it feels like you're the only one going through it, there are millions of people all over the world who have experienced something similar. The first step to overcoming it is acknowledging that it's real, even if your abuser tries to convince you otherwise. The next is to know that you are perfectly capable and deserving of honest and healthy relationships, and there are resources available to help you get there. Don't be afraid to reach out for support – you're stronger than you know!

CHAPTER 6:

THE DARK TRIAD

Have you ever heard of the dark personality traits that people with psychopathy and sociopathy carry? Such people are usually referred to as the Dark Triads! The name might sound a bit intimidating, and rightfully so, but there's often confusion about what it entails. It's not just a set of negative labels that are thrown around. In fact, scientific research has proven that individuals with these traits struggle with connecting to others in unique ways. Their self-perception sometimes conflicts with societal norms, and they have a harder time being agreeable, showing empathy, or putting others first.

The Dark Triad is a term used to describe three personality traits carried by people with narcissism, psychopathy, and Machiavellianism that are associated with negativity or malevolence. This term was coined in a 2002 study to better understand these traits. Interestingly, these traits all share a common core of low agreeableness, which can manifest as callousness or a willingness to exploit others. But did you know that these three personality traits aren't diagnosable mental health conditions alone? However, researchers have found clear links between narcissism and narcissistic personality disorder, as well as between psychopathy and antisocial personality disorder. Additionally, these traits share similarities with their respective disorders, but they aren't one and the same.

It's easy to get the three dark personalities confused, but it's important that you know there is a distinction between them. So, while there are certainly some overlapping characteristics, remember that narcissism, psychopathy, and antisocial personality disorder are unique in their own ways.

Have you ever noticed how some people exhibit similar but distinct personality traits that can be difficult to differentiate? It's crucial for you to be aware of these behaviors to avoid misidentifying one for the other. This can be especially tricky for those of us who aren't psychologists. Some traits can manifest as physical aggression while others rely on emotional manipulation. But don't worry, it's not uncommon to struggle with telling these personalities apart. A lot of research points to commonalities these behaviors share, but it's important to consider their impact on others. Most of the individuals who have one of the three personality traits from the Dark Triads tend to abuse people around them, which is why it's crucial to recognize and address these behaviors for the sake of everyone involved.

Narcissism

Have you ever met someone who just loves to talk about themselves and their achievements? Well, that's a trait commonly found in individuals with narcissism. We've talked much about narcissism, so we're familiar with this kind. We know narcissists have a strong desire to maintain a positive image and may even become defensive if they feel their reputation is being threatened. However, remember that while narcissists may come across as entitled or grandiose, they can also have vulnerabilities and struggles with self-esteem! In some cases, this may overlap with psychopathy.

Psychopathy

Different individuals possess varying levels of empathy and compassion. While some may naturally exhibit a stronger sense of care and concern for others, others struggle with these emotions. People with psychopathic tendencies, for example, have difficulty feeling a natural aversion to violence against others and not knowing the wrong with harming others. As a result, most psychopaths are considered cruel and aggressive.

Psychopathy also shares similarities with narcissism, but what distinguishes psychopathy from the rest of the dark triad is the exploitative nature of the condition. Ultimately, psychopathy is defined by ruthless selfishness and interpersonal boldness. As such, clinical psychology frameworks often use specific measures to diagnose the condition. Individuals with psychopathic tendencies often appear reckless or careless due to their willingness to take risks.

Machiavellianism

Machiavellians are known for their strategic approach to achieving their goals. They aren't motivated by their emotions or desires but rather by their long-term plans. And their focus on their agenda can sometimes lead them to make decisions that aren't in the best interest of others. While they may be less impulsive than others, they have been known to cheat or lie if it benefits them or if they believe they won't get caught. That being said, most people choose not to engage in dishonest behavior, but for Machiavellians, the decision ultimately comes down to whether it serves their interests and the potential consequences.

Identifying someone with a dark triad personality can be tricky since they often appear charismatic and charming. They are skilled at complimenting others and making them feel extra special. However, individuals with a dark triad personality cannot keep up this facade for long. Eventually, they'll exploit the people they've become close to, leading to burnt bridges and fractured relationships.

To help you spot someone with dark triad traits, keep an eye out for these four red flags:

1. Having difficulties maintaining relationships

Keeping long-lasting relationships can challenge most people with dark triad traits. This encompasses romantic partners, friends, family, and work colleagues. They may have encountered unsuccessful relationships in which they have unintentionally distanced themselves from significant people in their lives.

2. Thinking they are the victims

Some people with dark personality traits view themselves as victims in their relationships and life. Individuals with a dark triad personality are quite skilled at a pattern of behavior known as the narcissistic cycle of abuse and gaslighting. And when confronted, they flip the script and play the victim card. A study from 2019 found that those with narcissistic tendencies or diagnosed with narcissistic personality disorder are more likely to become aggressive or violent when they feel like they might be abandoned or their self-worth is in question.

3. Excessive need for fulfillment

Have you ever noticed that some people in your life seem to always be searching for something more, even at the cost of those around them? If this behavior comes in excessive or chronic form, chances are you're dealing with a narcissist or a psychopath. Always remember that if you're feeling drained or depleted in any way, you may be dealing with someone with a dark triad personality, someone who has a tendency to prioritize their own needs above all else.

Again, remember that it's super important to prioritize your own well-being. Don't hesitate to set boundaries to protect yourself from being taken advantage of.

4. Inconsistent stories

Sometimes, people with dark triad traits have trouble keeping their stories straight. They could be great at telling a tale to suit their needs, but their stories don't always match up over time. You might notice that some details seem inconsistent or don't quite add up. It's important to keep an open mind and pay attention to these little red flags as they come up.

Where Narcissism Stems From

Did you know that a person's upbringing and childhood environment could play a significant role in causing Narcissistic Personality Disorder? However, genetics may also have a hand in it. NPD can be challenging to understand, but we know that it mostly involves grandiosity, a strong craving for admiration, and difficulty relating to others.

If you have ever wondered what could cause someone to have a narcissistic personality disorder, the truth is that there isn't a confirmed cause. However, researchers have identified several potential factors that could contribute to it. It's not just one thing that can lead to NPD, but rather a combination of factors.

Let's talk about genetics first. Did you know that studies have shown that certain personality traits associated with NPD, such as entitlement and grandiosity, can actually be inherited? However, it's important to note that just because a parent has NPD, it doesn't necessarily mean their children will inherit the disorder. That being said, having a parent with NPD can increase the likelihood of their children developing it. Additionally, some individuals may have a genetic predisposition to NPD, which could put them at greater risk if they're exposed to certain factors.

Next comes parenting. Being a parent is a wonderful journey filled with ups and downs. Certain parenting behaviors may be linked to narcissistic personality disorder, but remember that not all parents who exhibit these behaviors do so with bad intentions.

For example, some studies indicate that overprotective parents may increase the risk of their child developing some type of narcissism, especially grandiose and vulnerable narcissism. Similarly, there's also a correlation between narcissistic personality disorder and overly lenient parents. Children receiving excessive praise or lacking boundaries are more likely to display traits associated with NPD later in life.

Let's talk about these parenting styles one by one and how they are linked with narcissism.

First up, we have authoritarian parenting. These parents try to control their children's behavior a bit too much and may not provide enough warmth, support, or open communication. They have high expectations for their children to follow the rules and achieve success, which can sometimes lead to children feeling like they need to be perfect to feel valued. However, if not approached with care, this can also lead to children feeling entitled or unloved.

These parents place a lot of emphasis on their child's achievements and adherence to rules. As a result, kids may feel the need to overvalue themselves in order to deal with this pressure. Additionally, they may adopt a sense of entitlement as a way to shield themselves from the feeling of being unappreciated or inadequate. And those are some of the defining traits of narcissism.

Next up, we have indulgent parenting. Have you ever heard that too much of a good thing can be bad? Well, that's true for parenting, too. When parents shower their children with constant praise and validation, it can actually have negative effects. While it's important to show your children love and support, it's also important to keep things in balance. By avoiding overindulgence, you can help your child develop a healthy sense of self-esteem without the risk of them developing a sense of entitlement.

If the child is given praise even when they didn't earn it or it is excessive, they may start to internalize how their parents view them and believe that they are much more special than the average person. If this continues, it's easy to see how such a kid could grow up to be a narcissist.

Lastly, we have neglectful parenting. It's when parents don't provide enough warmth and guidance to their children. They do not respond to their children's needs or validate their emotions. This can lead to children developing narcissistic traits as a way to cope with feeling neglected and unworthy.

At first glance, these parenting styles appear to be vastly dissimilar, but they could all potentially lead to the development of narcissism. The common thread among them is that none truly encourage a child to explore and cultivate their unique identity.

Too controlling parents can make it hard for their children to explore their own paths in life. As a result, these kids seek validation from external sources to feel good about themselves. Over time, this habit can lead to narcissism. On the other hand, parents who are too lenient might not set enough boundaries for their kids. Without proper guidance, children can develop unrealistic self-image and self-importance.

And when parents don't acknowledge their children's emotional needs, it can cause feelings of inadequacy and shame. These negative emotions might make some kids narcissistic and overcompensate for their perceived shortcomings. It's important to note that shame is a key factor in the development of vulnerable narcissism.

Being a parent significantly impacts children's lives, but remember that there's no magic formula for raising a narcissistic child. While some parenting techniques may contribute to this condition, it's important to understand that it's not solely the result of parenting behaviors. So, let's not blame ourselves or others for a disorder that involves a complex mix of factors.

A person's upbringing and cultural background can also influence the development of narcissism. People who have experienced maltreatment during childhood actually do have a higher risk of developing NPD in early adulthood. Narcissistic traits are also said to be more prevalent in individualistic cultures.

While parenting plays a significant role in a child's environment, other childhood experiences can also contribute to the likelihood of developing NPD. For instance, individuals who have experienced bullying for an extended period of time may exhibit narcissistic traits. Moreover, excessive criticism from parents or other adults, such as teachers, can also increase the risk of developing NPD.

Over the years, there have also been some interesting findings in the field of biology. It has been revealed that biological factors may play a role in the development of narcissism and NPD. Specifically, it has been found that individuals with NPD have higher levels of oxidative stress, which can negatively affect the body.

In addition, brain scans have revealed that those with NPD have less gray matter in the areas responsible for empathy. Neuroscientists have also discovered a connection between NPD and variations in prefrontal brain structure. While more research is needed, it's possible that in the future, we may be able to detect narcissistic personality traits just by studying someone's brain.

And that's not all! Some researchers have even hypothesized that physical appearance and attributes may contribute to the development of NPD. Traits such as athleticism, physical attractiveness, and strength have been linked to higher levels of narcissism.

Being in a Relationship with Dark Triads

Building healthy relationships is important for our well-being. But what's even more important is to be cautious about who you let into your life. People with the dark triad personality will never have your best interests at heart. So, while they may seem charming and friendly, they are hardwired to exploit others. Whether it's a friend, coworker, family member, or partner, you must be mindful of their behavior. It's important to prioritize our own well-being and set boundaries if necessary.

Of course, we can't completely rule out the idea that someone with a dark triad personality could potentially change. However, it's important to remember that the odds of this happening are too low and may not be worth investing too much energy into. This is because the traits that make up this personality type are quite deep-rooted, making change difficult.

If you come across someone who exhibits dark triad personality traits, it's best to distance yourself as much as possible for your own well-being. However, if you find yourself in a situation where you're unsure if someone you're interacting with has these traits or if you're unable to just walk away, don't hesitate to contact a counselor or therapist for assistance. They can help you navigate the situation with compassion and understanding.

A relationship with any of these three types would include a lot of lies. We all want to be honest and trustworthy, but people with dark triad personality traits are prone to lying. They tend to lie more frequently and even think they're good at it. Those with Machiavellian tendencies tend to tell more white lies, while narcissistic individuals are more likely to exaggerate their popularity or status. And people with high levels of psychopathy often lie for no apparent reason!

Building trust in a relationship is crucial, but it can be tough when your partner constantly lies to you. Sometimes, you might get a sense that things aren't adding up or catch them in a little fib. Even harmless lies can hint at insincerity; repeated instances can lead to doubts about your security. To make matters worse, people with high scores on the dark triad personality scale are also more likely to cheat on their partners.

It's not really a shocker since they tend to be impulsive, less concerned about others' feelings, and pretty good at lying. But what's really fascinating is how different traits within the dark triad can lead to different types of infidelity.

When someone with a higher level of psychopathy cheats, it often leads to a breakup. On the other hand, those who are more Machiavellian in nature seem to be able to keep the relationship going even after cheating. Perhaps this is because their strategic mindset allows them to avoid getting caught. Even if they are discovered, they are skilled at talking their way out of trouble by manipulating their partner. The same goes for narcissists, who either deny any cheating or find a way to shift all the blame onto you.

Please remember that if your partner is caught cheating with someone else and tries to blame you for being too overbearing, it's not your fault. Don't be deceived by their manipulation tactics - this is just classic Machiavellian behavior at play.

Did you know that most people who cheat are actually more likely to be suspicious of their partner cheating on them, too? And if they also have the dark triad personality traits, it makes them feel jealous even when there's no reason to be. Moreover, they tend to act out in revenge if they get cheated on, like yelling or spreading rumors about their partner.

According to a study, women with the dark triad personality traits admitted wanting revenge but not necessarily wanting to end the relationship even if their partner cheated. It seems like they crave emotional control over their partner rather than simply acting out impulsively.

The dark triads also often prefer more superficial relationships. This isn't to say that short-term flings or casual dating isn't fun and totally okay! We all have different needs at different times in our lives, and sometimes we just want to keep things light and easy. But people who possess darker triad traits often prefer relationships that lack emotional depth, whether romantic or platonic. Narcissistic individuals tend to have a one-night-stand approach, while those with psychopathic traits may prefer flings.

In terms of friendships, Machiavellians tend to seek out people with high social status, while narcissists prefer to be a part of a group with good looks. Meanwhile, men with psychopathic traits seek friends who can assist them in pursuing potential partners.

When it comes to dealing with individuals who exhibit dark triad behavior, the best approach is to steer clear of any interactions with them. It's important to remember that trying to change their perspective or convince them of anything may prove to be an uphill battle. Instead, focus on surrounding yourself with positive, uplifting people who appreciate and value you for who you are. This can make a world of difference in your overall well-being and happiness.

CHAPTER 7:

NARCISSISTIC TACTICS

Being in a relationship with a narcissist can be quite confusing and saddening. It can be tough to understand why they behave the way they do. Emotional abuse is their way of manipulating and controlling you, making you feel less confident and impacting your mental wellness. But don't worry; there are ways to overcome this and regain your sense of self-worth, starting with being aware of the tactics they use.

In healthy relationships, both parties strive to support each other and contribute to mutual happiness. Narcissists, however, use manipulative tactics to maintain power over their partners. This can leave the other person feeling confused, invalidated, and emotionally exhausted. These tactics include gaslighting, which distorts your reality and makes you doubt your memory and sanity. Other manipulative tactics include belittling, criticizing, and mocking, making you feel inadequate. Some people use silent treatment to punish or control their partner, causing anxiety. Additionally, they may restrict your connections with others, making you feel dependent on them. Emotional blackmail, including threats of self-harm or relationship damage, is another tool used to force compliance.

Recognizing these tactics and seeking support if you've experienced them is important. Healthy relationships are built on mutual respect, trust, and open communication. Let's talk about some of the narcissistic tactics in detail:

Belittling

Being in a relationship with a narcissist can really take a toll on your emotional well-being. Sometimes, after the initial honeymoon phase, narcissists tend to enter a phase where they start to criticize, ignore, or belittle their partners. This can slowly lower your self-esteem and sense of worth. Following the devaluation phase, there comes a time when the narcissist decides to end the relationship or withdraw their affection suddenly. This can leave you feeling unsure and hurt, and the sudden breakup can be unbearable.

Relationships with narcissists always make you go through a really tough time. You soon begin to notice that your partner or friend has started to become more distant and critical toward you. It can be difficult to deal with when they belittle your interests and even insult your appearance. It is always such a big change from the loving and attentive person you first met!

Then, out of nowhere, they might even end things with you! It can be really sudden, and narcissists don't like to offer any explanations in this case. And you're left alone, feeling totally confused and hurt. You can't help but wonder if you have done something wrong. You can't help but blame yourself for the relationship ending.

It's super important to understand that when it comes to narcissistic manipulation, the phase of extreme love and affection can quickly turn into belittling, leading to the narcissist discarding you. Just keep in mind that these stages are all about the narcissist's own insecurities and their extreme need for control. It is in no way a reflection of your worth or value. If you've been through a relationship like this, you have to promote healing through self-care and self-love. The negative image of you that the narcissist created is not real. You have your own value and worth.

Hoovering

Hoovering is a term used to describe a behavior that some people exhibit after a disagreement or separation in a relationship. They might try to win their partner back with promises of change, affection, guilt trips, or even material things.

Narcissists are usually guilty of this and always make you hope things will improve. They will apologize and try to make things right by showering you with love and affection. Sometimes, they may even play the victim and claim that they can't manage to live without you. But it's all a part of their manipulation and narcissistic tactics.

Remember that although some manipulative behaviors may change temporarily, they often resurface again, leaving individuals feeling emotionally drained and confused. However, if you recognize the hoovering technique, you can resist the urge to get back into the cycle of abuse. Just remember that real change takes time and effort, and it's not your responsibility to take care of or always be there for your narcissistic partner or friend.

Silent Treatment

Have you ever experienced a situation where your partner suddenly stops talking to you or showing affection? This behavior, known as the silent treatment, is a common tactic narcissist's use. They use it to punish their partners for things they perceive as wrong or to make them comply with their wishes. Unfortunately, this can make their partners anxious, confused, and desperate. It's important to communicate openly and honestly in any relationship, so if you are on the receiving end of the silent treatment, don't hesitate to reach out for support instead of bearing it silently.

Feeling ignored or shut out by someone you care about is never a pleasant experience. If you disagree with them or don't meet their expectations, narcissists like to give you the silent treatment for hours or even days. This, in turn, makes you feel confused and anxious, unsure of what you have done wrong or how to make things right. The silent treatment can be tough because it goes against our natural desire for connection and communication. It makes us feel invisible and unworthy, leaving us desperate to reconcile.

By recognizing this tactic and understanding that everyone deserves to express their thoughts and feelings without fear of being ignored or dismissed, you can take the first step in breaking its hold on you. Don't let anyone make you feel like your emotions are invalid. You are entitled to your opinions and feelings, which should be respected. Remember this and don't be afraid to stand up for yourself!

Isolating

Maintaining healthy relationships with friends and family is important, but sometimes things can get complicated when you are in a narcissistic relationship. Narcissists often try to isolate their partners from their support networks. It can start off subtly, with small comments here and there, but over time it can escalate to the point where the partner feels guilty for spending time with loved ones.

If you're in a relationship with a narcissist, they might have said negative things about your friends or become upset when you see them. Eventually, this can make you start avoiding your loved ones altogether, just to avoid conflict. It's a tough situation to be in, but remember that healthy relationships involve mutual respect and trust.

Being isolated by a narcissistic partner can leave you feeling more dependent on them and less likely to seek outside opinions. That's why it's crucial to maintain your relationships and support networks. These connections can provide you with a fresh perspective, emotional support, and a helping hand when things start to feel overwhelming. So don't be afraid to lean on your loved ones - they're here for you!

If you ever feel like your relationship is causing you to drift away from people you care about, it's a good idea to take a moment to reflect on why that might be happening. After all, a happy relationship should add to your life, not isolate you from the important people in it. Remember that it's always worth examining how your relationships affect you and making adjustments as necessary.

Emotional Blackmail

Narcissists often use emotional manipulation to get what they want. This means that they try to make their significant other feel guilty, scared, or obligated to do what they want. It can be subtle, or it can be more obvious threats.

For example, a narcissist would often say, "I've done so much for you, and this is how you treat me?" or "If you really loved me, you wouldn't do this." These kinds of statements can make you feel guilty, and you could feel like you have to do what your partner wants, even when it isn't the best thing for you. Needless to say, this kind of emotional blackmail can really take a toll on your mental health. It can make you feel guilty and anxious and can even damage your self-esteem.

This form of manipulation often preys on a person's insecurities and fears, making it especially harmful. In a healthy relationship, respecting each other's boundaries and feelings is important. Partners shouldn't resort to guilt trips or threats just to get what they want. By recognizing emotional blackmail for what it is, you can take a big step in regaining control of your autonomy and self-esteem in a relationship with someone who may have narcissistic tendencies.

Projection

Have you ever noticed that some people tend to shift the blame onto others when things go wrong? It's a common habit, especially among those with narcissistic tendencies. Rather than taking responsibility for their actions, they resort to projection as a defense mechanism. This means they attribute their shortcomings or negative emotions to their partner instead of acknowledging their role in the situation. Remember, everyone makes mistakes and has flaws, and a healthy relationship involves taking responsibility for our own behavior and emotions.

Narcissists can just never admit when they were wrong. They like to shift the blame onto others rather than take responsibility for their actions. Narcissists love to behave badly and then turn it around to make it seem like it was your fault instead. It can be really frustrating to deal with their constant projection and blame-shifting. It can make you feel like you are the root of all their problems, leading to feelings of guilt and shame.

Victims of narcissistic abuse need to understand that they are not to blame. When a narcissist refuses to take responsibility for their actions, it's more a reflection of their own inadequacies rather than anything their partner has done wrong. Keep this in mind, and stay strong.

Triangulation

Triangulation is when someone brings a third person into a situation to create a sense of unease or to make themselves look better. For example, they might talk to someone else in front of their partner, compare their partner to an ex negatively, or use another person's opinion to make their partner doubt their own thoughts or feelings. It's a very common tactic employed by narcissists, and it can cause a lot of hurt and confusion for the victim.

Your partner or friend with narcissistic tendencies could have a habit of bringing up their previous partners or other friends to compare them to you. They might say things like, "Oh, my ex was always so much better at cooking than you," or "My friend is so much more adventurous than you." If this continues, it's normal to start feeling insecure about everything. You wouldn't want to feel like you are constantly competing with someone who isn't even in the picture anymore.

Have you ever talked with someone where you share your thoughts and feelings, only to have them dismissed because of someone else's opinion? Unfortunately, narcissists love to do that by using their friends' opinions to counter their concerns. Instead of validating your feelings, they say things like, "My friends don't think it's a big deal," which can leave you feeling unheard and disrespected.

Using triangulation in a relationship can make you feel insecure and create a sense of unhealthy competition. Sadly, narcissists who use this tactic are doing it to maintain control and keep their partner always seeking their approval. If you've been through something like this, know that your feelings and perspective are always valid, no matter what someone else might try to make you think. By recognizing these manipulative behaviors, you can take steps to protect yourself.

Blocking

You might have experienced situations where the narcissist suddenly stops communicating with you. This behavior is known as stonewalling, and it often happens when a narcissist is involved. One of the ways it can manifest is through blocking.

It's important to remember that this isn't necessarily about you. Narcissists may block you to boost their own sense of power and control. They want to feel important and valued, and blocking you gives them a sense of validation. Essentially, the narcissist decides to block you on all real-time and verbal communication platforms such as social media, instant messaging, and phone calls.

The reason behind this behavior is that narcissists crave attention, validation, and admiration. By blocking you, they create a situation where you are constantly trying to reach out to them, making them feel important and special. They may even want you to create new social media accounts or go through friends and family just to communicate with them.

It's important to remember that this behavior is unhealthy and should not be tolerated. No one should make you feel like you need to chase them or go to great lengths just to communicate with them.

But that's not always the reason why they do this. Sometimes, when the narcissist feels challenged, they also resort to blocking. They might set up a situation to make you frustrated, annoyed, or defensive just so they can get a reaction out of you. But then, when you're about to respond, they block you, so you can't say anything back.

Trauma Bond Healing

A trauma bond is when a strong connection forms between someone who has been hurt and the person who caused the harm; in this case, between a narcissist and their victim. Unfortunately, this bond is really damaging, with many ups and downs. To cope with this challenging situation, survivors of trauma often become very aware of the actions, words, and desires of their abuser. Over time, this can lead to the survivor losing touch with their own sense of self, as well as their own needs and values.

Did you know that the dopamine and cortisol levels in your brain can take up to 9-12 weeks to stabilize after experiencing ups and downs? But don't worry; with the help of a therapist, you can navigate through the healing process much quicker! It's important to know that there's no set time for your brain to steady off, but with the right support, you can overcome any challenges you've been carrying around in your subconscious.

The first stage of healing from the trauma bond is to remember and recognize the seven tactics that an abuser might try to control their victim:

Gaslighting

As your relationship with the narcissist grows, you may gradually become aware of things that make you feel uneasy. For example, whenever you try to talk about problems or express your emotions, your partner frequently contradicts or distorts the facts. This can make you doubt your own memory and perceptions, which is a technique called gaslighting often employed by narcissists to manipulate their partners.

Gaslighting is a sneaky tactic that can come in many different forms. It's when someone tries to manipulate the truth by denying certain facts or changing the story. Sometimes it can be as simple as denying that they said something hurtful or claiming that an event happened differently than how their partner remembers it. But over time, this can really wear a person down and make them doubt themselves.

For example, your narcissistic partner made a mean comment about your appearance, but when you bring it up with them, they deny it completely and even accuse you of trying to start a fight. If this keeps repeating, you will naturally feel confused and wonder if your memory is accurate.

It's normal for victims to feel really confused and unsure of themselves when they're being gaslit. It's a tricky way for someone to try and control another person because it makes them doubt their own thoughts and feelings. All of the doubt is directed to themselves instead of the narcissist. But remember, trusting your instincts is always important!

Love Bombing

From the moment I met my partner, I was completely smitten by his charm and the way he adored me. He was everything I had ever hoped for – attentive, affectionate, and utterly in love with me. Little did I know, it's a common trick known as love bombing, a phase where narcissists will do everything in their power to win over their target. They will shower their partner with compliments, gifts, and love, making you believe you have found the perfect partner for yourself.

For the narcissist, showering someone with affection can actually let them have the upper hand. Firstly, it makes that person feel incredibly special and loved, and secondly, it creates a sense of closeness and dependence, making it harder for them to imagine life without their partner. The victim, looking back at their relationship romance, might remember how flattered they were by their partner's constant attention. Of course, it can be really sweet to feel adored and loved. But this very thing, unfortunately, makes it tough for them to spot the manipulation and control that comes later.

However, once you grasp and understand this tactic, it can be a major turning point for you. You can see that your relationship isn't picture-perfect like you thought. Instead, you will recognize that you are trapped in a pattern of manipulation that began with the love-bombing phase.

Emotional Addiction

Living with a narcissist will eventually make you get emotionally attached to them. The narcissist has played mind games, and you're now so reliant on them that you can't imagine life without them. They've created a toxic atmosphere where you feel like you can't be yourself or leave the relationship. Once you reach this point, you might forget about your career, friends, and other relationships, and you might feel like you're living solely for their approval or disapproval, likes and dislikes.

It's totally understandable to feel drawn to the anticipation and connection you feel with someone, even if it's not always a healthy relationship. The human brain is wired to seek out pleasure and reward, which can sometimes lead us down the wrong path. But did you know that the chemicals released in our brains during emotional addiction are similar to those released when we consume drugs or alcohol? Both emotional and substance addiction are linked to dopamine release in the brain.

While emotional addiction can make it hard to let go of someone who may not be treating you well, substance addiction involves cravings and withdrawal symptoms. So, while they share some similarities, they are also quite different.

Remember, seeking help is a brave and important step in breaking free from any unhealthy patterns in your life.

Criticism

It's not always easy to notice the subtle changes that can happen in a relationship. In normal and healthy relationships, as two people get closer, becoming more comfortable with each other can feel like a natural progression. But narcissists shift to criticism and devaluation instead. They start to belittle you or blame you for things that aren't your fault. This can be hurtful and confusing, especially if it seems to come out of nowhere. As the relationship progresses, they might become more demanding or seem impossible to please.

During this stage, the narcissist will start to criticize and invalidate you, making you feel like you don't matter. It's understandable to feel confused and unsure about your thoughts and feelings due to the manipulative tactics being used against you, but if you feel like you're becoming more and more dependent on someone who may be harming you, it's time to take a step back and evaluate the situation.

It's okay to take time to process what's happening and seek support from trusted friends or professionals. Remember, your thoughts and emotions are valid, and it's important to break free from any negative beliefs that may have been forced upon you.

Loss of Self-Trust and Dependency

As the narcissist continues to manipulate you, you will begin to feel a strong connection to them. They may shower you with affection and words of praise, making you feel cherished and valued. However, it's important to be aware that your feelings are being manipulated as your partner tries to influence your thoughts and emotions slowly but surely. This is all for you to start to feel dependent on them.

You will often find yourself in tricky situations with a narcissist who will deliberately try to embarrass you in front of your loved ones. It can be pretty uncomfortable and downright unfair when they cause a scene to make you appear in a negative light to your friends and family. The best way to tackle this is by remaining calm and not reacting to their behavior. I know it's tough to resist the urge to retaliate, but remember that reacting only fuels their manipulative tendencies.

Do you know about "Dog Whistling"? It's a term that can help you recognize covert emotional abuse in public. Basically, when someone uses specific phrases or looks that only you understand, it can be a subtle way to manipulate and devalue you. For instance, if you're sensitive about your weight, they might compliment someone else while giving you a sideways glance. And if you react, they will blame you and call you crazy or jealous. The goal is to trigger you and make you feel like you're the problem. But again, the best thing you can do is stay in control and not give them the reaction they want.

Resigning to Control

In the end, you feel like you just can't seem to get through to your partner no matter how hard you try. You find yourself feeling helpless and giving up on trying to improve your situation. This usually happens when you have been facing abuse for quite some time and feel like you cannot do anything to change it.

There are many reasons why you may feel this way. One reason could be that you believe you do not deserve better treatment. You might think you are not good enough or have made a mistake, and therefore feel you must accept the abuse. But that's not true! No matter what kind of relationship you are in, safety and respect should be there from both sides!

It's unfortunate, but sometimes victims of abuse do feel trapped in their relationship. They may be afraid of their abuser or feel like they have no one to turn to because they've been cut off from friends and family. Abusers can be really good at manipulating and threatening their victims to keep them from leaving. Another thing to watch out for is the feeling that you're the only one who can help your abuser. It's natural to want to take care of the people we love, but sometimes that impulse can put us in danger.

It's tough when you're in a relationship with a narcissist because having a logical and open discussion just seems impossible. Instead of resolving conflict, you find yourself feeling drained and frustrated. You may even feel like you have to do things their way just to keep the peace, which isn't fair to you or your boundaries. It's important to remember that compromising your values isn't the answer.

If you're in a situation where you feel like you can't leave or you're trying to "save" your abuser, know that there are resources available to help you. You don't have to go through this alone.

Going through traumatic experiences with a narcissist is undoubtedly tough, but it's not just about surviving the initial event. You have to deal with flashbacks, panic attacks, and other challenges like PTSD and hypervigilance. It's important to remember that these feelings can linger for a while and really impact your life. But don't worry! You will heal and learn to manage these emotions. It may not happen overnight, but with time and effort, you'll learn to control them and move forward. So, keep fighting and keep healing!

CHAPTER 8:

NARCISSISTS SPLITTING

Each one of us is unique and has different aspects of our personality. However, these facets can be more intense and inflexible for individuals with narcissistic personality disorder. One characteristic of this disorder is narcissistic splitting, wherein a person views themselves and others in extremes, either as entirely good or entirely bad.

If someone has a strong sense of self, they're able to see that there's both good and bad in the world and that sometimes those two things can even overlap. They know that when something bad happens, it doesn't mean that all the good disappears. In fact, both good and bad can exist simultaneously in a person or situation without causing any instability. However, certain individuals like those with narcissistic tendencies find it challenging to balance the good and bad aspects of a situation. This can lead to what is called "splitting," where they struggle to unite the different components of the situation. Instead, they tend to compartmentalize everything into either the "good" or "bad" category. So, it can be tough for them to appreciate things in a more nuanced way.

When it comes to people with narcissism, they tend to view themselves as flawless and without fault, while others fall short and are unworthy. This mindset can present some challenges when it comes to forming positive relationships, as they struggle to see people as anything more than a means of validation or a threat to their ego. In the eyes of a narcissist, things are either good or bad, right or wrong, with little room for gray areas or complexity. As a result, they have trouble empathizing with others or considering different perspectives outside of their own. Additionally, they react defensively to criticism or perceived slights, making it difficult to regulate their emotions.

Splitting is actually a defense mechanism that narcissists use to avoid feeling uncomfortable when good and bad things happen at the same time. Essentially, when someone splits, they're able to separate these two opposing ideas and maintain their sense of self without feeling overwhelmed. This coping mechanism helps them preserve their sense of self-importance by projecting their negative traits onto others.

It's not uncommon for people with certain personality traits to experience what's known as splitting. This simply means that they tend to see things in very black-and-white terms, with little room for shades of gray. But this behavior isn't limited to just personality disorders - it can crop up in other mental health conditions, too.

Just like no two snowflakes are alike, the symptoms and signs of splitting behaviors can vary from person to person. Here are some common ones you may come across:

Sudden and extreme shifts in how they feel about or perceive someone.

Sometimes, you might notice the narcissist idolizing someone one minute and then feeling frustrated with them the next. It makes it hard to understand whether they like the person in question or dislike them. It can be incredibly frustrating and confusing, but narcissists, as we know, tend to put people on a pedestal and idolize them at first, but as soon as that person does something they don't like or doesn't live up to their expectations, they quickly turn on them. No matter how good they were, now that they've done some wrong according to the narcissist, the latter can never see them as a good person anymore.

Struggling to view things in shades of gray.

It can be tough for narcissists to see all the subtle shades of gray in a situation. It's important to take a step back and appreciate the nuances and complexities that make up our world. There's always more than meets the eye! However narcissists are unable to take a step back and appreciate the complexities and nuances of the world. And since they can't look at things and situations from different angles and perspectives that also adds to their lack of understanding and empathy toward others. They limit their sight and brain to the two extremes only.

Having difficulty in sustaining steady connections.

Splitting can sometimes pose a challenge in cultivating and nurturing positive relationships, which is why most narcissists don't have stable relationships. They constantly switch between idealizing and devaluing the other person, seeing them as either perfect or deeply flawed. Ultimately, this makes it difficult for narcissists to form meaningful and lasting relationships.

Struggling with self-image.

Since splitting divides behavior into completely good or bad, narcissists find it hard to form a stable self-image and even feel insecure about themselves. The constant back and forth leaves them confused about who they are or how they should view themselves. Of course, narcissists will always think highly of themselves on the surface, but it doesn't mean they don't feel insecure or don't struggle with self-doubt. Their splitting behavior makes it hard for them to reconcile with their own flaws and mistakes.

Inability to see both the positive and negative sides of a person or situation.

Narcissists with splitting behavior tend to view the world through a narrow lens, seeing things very polarized. They don't see the shades of gray in life; to them, everything is all good or bad. This is why narcissists find it tricky to find the silver lining in a not-so-great situation or to identify positive areas in a negative situation. They also fail to recognize areas that could use improvement within a positive circumstance. For example, if they receive constructive criticism, they see it as a personal attack and become defensive, rather than considering it as an opportunity for growth. On the other hand, if they receive praise, they may become overly confident and dismiss any potential areas for improvement.

Intense emotional reactions that seem disproportionate to the situation at hand.

Narcissists often seem to overreact to things while sometimes dismissing or completely ignoring a situation. This is because they see others as "good" people and "bad people". If you've been extremely patient with a narcissist and you lose your cool only one time, that one time will make you the bad person from a narcissist's viewpoint, regardless of how many other times you have been good to them. So, when you do something that doesn't fit into their perfect angel image, they will react with extreme anger and disappointment, even if it is something insignificant. This can be extremely confusing and exhausting because you can never predict how they will react in any given situation.

Hard to make rational decisions during challenging times.

Narcissists struggle with decision-making for this very reason - that they only see things in two extremes, without any middle ground. So, when they are faced with a complex situation, they don't know how to weigh the pros and cons, the good and bad, to make a rational decision. They find it hard to balance the two sides and make thoughtful decisions.

Feeling empty or disintegrated inside.

The splitting behavior of narcissists that you can only be either all good or all bad ends up applying to them too! And since many narcissists struggle with deep-seated insecurity and low self-esteem, they struggle with feelings of emptiness and inner turmoil that they cover with their outward displays of confidence and self-importance. In an attempt to compensate for these feelings, they engage in self-promotion, attention-seeking behaviors, and manipulation of others to maintain their sense of superiority and control. Even so, there's no excuse for their abusive and manipulative behavior.

Did you know that splitting is a common phenomenon that also occurs in personality disorders apart from Narcissistic Personality Disorder, such as Borderline Personality Disorder and Histrionic Personality Disorder? It creates extreme polarization in perceptions of individuals and relationships and hinders them from forming meaningful and healthy connections. While there are plenty of treatment options available for them, it ultimately falls on them to seek treatment. Narcissists, sadly, would never go out of their way to understand or even acknowledge that they have a disorder, much less look for ways to get support and help to better themselves.

Black and White Thinking

An important part of splitting is black-and-white thinking, which is essentially the same thing. Narcissists struggle with seeing the good in something they consider bad, and vice versa. It's more common for those who struggle with pathological narcissism. They tend to have a tough time with conflicting emotions and can't seem to sustain them. For example, they can't be upset with someone and still see the positive qualities in them. They also can't accept someone's flaws or mistakes while still liking them. This way of thinking is very extreme, but it's just one of the reasons why even narcissists struggle to deal with themselves.

Their way of viewing things is really unique, but not in a good way. For example, if a narcissist likes something, it doesn't just stop at "liking" – they will be head over heels for it. Similarly, disliking something for them means that they can't stand it at all. And when they are faced with disappointment, it feels like the end of the world to them. They also have a hard time knowing how to differentiate between emotions, which often leads to extreme reactions from them. These reactions can be hard for those around them to understand. Sometimes, their emotions can be so overwhelming that they overreact, while at other times, they seem completely disconnected.

This kind of black-and-white thinking is not just tough for the narcissist but everyone involved, especially their victims.

People who are not narcissists also sometimes think in black and white, but that can be really limiting and not entirely accurate. This type of thinking goes hand in hand with other cognitive distortions like filtering and disqualifying the positives in a situation.

113

When we filter, we are ignoring the good things that don't fit into our narrative, and disqualifying the positives involves rejecting and reframing these good things to fit into our preconceived notions.

So, when you do nice things for your narcissistic friend or partner and they suddenly turn on you for the one "wrong" you did, all the good things that you've done are either forgotten or dismissed as insignificant. Even worse, the narcissist may twist your actions to fit their negative perception of you. This can be incredibly hurtful and frustrating because it feels like nothing you do is ever good enough for them or safe for you.

This is one of the major reasons why dealing with narcissists is so challenging. They just keep viewing everything through their current perception of you, which is often negative.

Let's talk about love bombing now - when the narcissist decides to shower you with excessive affection and admiration. Sure, it can be flattering at first, but it's also a form of black-and-white thinking! It's when they see you as all-good. Unfortunately, this type of cognitive distortion almost always results in a lack of stability and security within the relationship. Having a sense of consistency in any relationship is important, but with love bombers and narcissists, you can never count on things staying the same.

So, splitting is just another way our brains process information and emotions. Black and white thinking is when we see things as completely good or bad. It is a defense mechanism that is often seen in narcissists. When they are faced with emotional contradictions, they struggle to understand how a good person could do something bad and vice versa. This then creates a conflict in their minds that they don't know how to resolve.

To make sense of it all, they start to "split" the person or situation into two separate parts – the good and the bad. This allows their brain to process the information in a way that makes sense to them. It is one of the ways we can see how narcissists are so immature, especially in emotional aspects. They just want to hold onto one extreme aspect of a person or situation while completely ignoring the other. Ultimately, this leads to all kinds of problems and conflicts.

You can sometimes observe a distinct duality in how narcissists interact with others and how they present themselves. They may showcase an extreme version of themselves that seems entirely separate from their usual behavior, leaving those around them confused and unsure how to process it all. It's easy for our brains to want to categorize and understand what we're seeing, but when the behavior is so vastly contrasting, it can be difficult to reconcile. As a result, the victim may end up engaging in black-and-white thinking of their own, creating multiple categories to try to make sense of what they're seeing. It's a complex phenomenon, but one that's important to recognize and understand. Basically, you start thinking and seeing in extremes too, influenced by the narcissist's behavior.

This is the only thing narcissists and victims experience in a similar way. You see, narcissists are often hard to categorize and don't fit neatly into boxes. This can be confusing for their victims, especially since most people don't think in extremes like black and white. At times, the differing emotions and information surrounding a narcissist can leave victims feeling confused and conflicted. In order to make sense of these contradictions, it's common for them to create a separate category just for them.

One example of this is that you start believing that narcissists are not quite human, which can be a way to protect your own sense of self and preserve a positive view of humanity. However, it's important to remember that people with narcissistic tendencies are still people, even if their behavior is difficult to understand. Acknowledging this can be challenging, but it's ultimately a step toward healing and growing from the abuse you have been subjected to.

It's understandable that some victims become uneasy at the thought of humanizing narcissists. How can such a cruel and apathetic person be human? This is likely due to a fear that recognizing the humanity in such people would reopen your old wounds or create sympathy for them when they don't deserve it. But they're still people, no matter how mean and abusive they are.

Every person, even narcissists and those with similar traits and disorders has gone through complex experiences that contribute to their behavior. Understanding and acknowledging this doesn't mean you are excusing their abuse or harmful actions. It just means you are recognizing the full range of human experience. You can still protect yourself while also seeing the humanity in others. It's how you grow and heal.

It's a fact that people with pathological narcissism are different from those who don't exhibit such behavior. However, let's not forget that narcissism is something very human as we're all driven by our egos. Remember, we all could have some level of narcissistic traits in us. So, it's possible for some of these behaviors to surface in anyone, regardless of whether they are a narcissist or not.

While it may seem necessary to distance yourself from this aspect of humanity when you are healing, it's not a good idea as it makes you more vulnerable to these traits in others and yourself. So, let's embrace humanity and remember that we're all a work in progress!

Again, I don't mean that you have to excuse narcissistic or abusive behavior. Never do that! But letting go of the belief that these people aren't human doesn't mean they are good people. They should still be held responsible for their actions. Refusing to understand or acknowledge such humans could trigger black-and-white thinking in you too, which we know is not a good thing. It's how you identify and resolve your emotional blind spots.

However, it's totally understandable why victims in narcissistic relationships struggle with seeing things in black and white. Our brains have a funny way of trying to protect us, even in situations that are really difficult. It's like we try to deny or reframe the bad stuff so we can justify staying with someone who we know deep down isn't good for us. That's what we all do. That's what keeps us in the relationship for so long. When you finally think of leaving, it's not only the narcissist stopping you but your own black-and-white thinking that you've developed along the way too!

But here's the thing: you don't have to keep playing that game. You can learn to evaluate things in a more balanced and realistic way, and you have to remember that no amount of good behavior or past trauma can ever excuse abuse. Sure, narcissists may have had a difficult childhood, but so what? That doesn't allow them to treat YOU like that. And it doesn't obligate you to understand their origin, excuse their behavior, or try to help them.

Here's some comforting news: If you're not a narcissist, chances are you can easily correct any cognitive distortions you may have by simply checking in with reality. Whereas, for narcissists, their unique relationship with reality makes this process much more challenging. It's next to impossible for them to incorporate new information into their beliefs and perceptions, which can cause some of the issues they face.

Do you know that feeling when you're stuck between a rock and a hard place? That's cognitive dissonance. Sometimes, we just can't seem to make sense of conflicting thoughts or beliefs. And often, we're unsure whether someone we know is good or bad. But guess what? People aren't that simple. We all have the capacity for good and bad, and that's okay! Instead of trying to categorize others, let's focus on their actions. After all, actions speak louder than words. And that's how we can get rid of black-and-white thinking.

Looking at things from a wider angle, it's unsafe to assume that humans are always good and kind. We can't just brush off someone's bad actions by saying they aren't human. It's a trap to think that people who look or act a certain way won't do something terrible. We've all seen that this isn't the case. When we agreed to get into a relationship with the narcissist, we never knew things would turn out this way.

Being in a relationship with a narcissist is never easy. It can be tricky to navigate their world, but with some effort and understanding, you'll get there. You might feel like you have to watch your words and actions all the time but try to remember that their reactions are not your fault. It's like walking on a tightrope, but know that you can always reach out for support if you need it.

It's also important to understand that when someone engages in narcissistic splitting, it's not their fault - it's a symptom of a personality disorder. That being said, it's also crucial to prioritize your well-being and protect yourself from harmful behavior. This could mean seeking out therapy for yourself or even encouraging your loved one to seek professional help. Remember, taking care of yourself is always a top priority!

Remember that splitting is a way for people with a narcissistic personality disorder to keep their self-esteem sky-high. But it also creates a world where everything is super polarized - totally amazing or awful. It can be tough to navigate a relationship with someone who does this, but learning about this coping mechanism can help. You're not to blame for their behavior, and there's help out there for you!

CHAPTER 9:

SELF-LOVE

Growing up in an abusive environment can make self-love seem like a challenging concept. If the people in your life are always pointing out your flaws and using them as an excuse to be angry with you, it's natural to wonder whether it's okay to love yourself. You may have even been punished for trying to set boundaries, which can make you feel like self-love is a dangerous thing. Also, if you grew up with a narcissistic parent, you may have learned that your needs don't matter and that taking care of yourself is selfish. But don't worry, it's never too late to learn how to love yourself and put your own needs first.

You've been through so much in your life. When a narcissist picks you up as their victim, you learn to motivate yourself through criticism and fear. If you were in contact with a narcissist as a child or teenager, their abuse may have taught your brain to always be in survival mode. And unfortunately, the narcissist's hurtful words can become the foundation of your inner critic, which is your way of protecting yourself from further harm. Then, you start to devalue yourself just like the narcissist does.

While these experiences can make you become an expert at keeping yourself safe, you might not have learned how to truly love, value, and care for yourself. But you know what? It's never too late to start! You are worthy of all the care and love in the world, and I'm here to support you along the way.

Importance of Self-Love

Did you know that not loving yourself can actually make you more vulnerable to abusive behavior from loved ones? Without a healthy dose of self-love, setting boundaries and prioritizing your time and resources can be tough. Plus, neglecting your physical and mental health can have serious consequences. But don't worry! By practicing self-love, you can protect yourself from harm and live your best life. It will make you stronger and more resilient. And it can even help decrease stress and boost your immune system.

When we practice self-love and compassion, we're more likely to bounce back from tough times and find happiness in the long run. Feeling good about ourselves also helps us remember our humanity, which is especially important for survivors of narcissistic abuse. Sadly, abusers often try to make their victims feel worthless and less than human. But when we love and value ourselves, we know that we deserve better than that. Practicing self-love and compassion can help us conquer these negative beliefs.

By loving yourself and being kind to yourself, you can start to see your experiences as part of the bigger picture of being human, rather than feeling alone and isolated. By being mindful of your thoughts and feelings instead of getting wrapped up in them, you can learn to deal with them in a healthier way.

Practicing Self-Love

Going through a relationship with a narcissistic abuser can be a really hard experience and it can leave a lasting impact on your life, no matter how long you were together. After such a relationship ends, it can be really challenging to get back to valuing and loving yourself. If you find yourself feeling stuck and helpless, don't worry - you're not alone!

Let's keep showing ourselves some love and remember how amazing and worthy we truly are!

Below are some tips to practice so you can start to take back control of your life and feel like yourself again in no time:

It starts with self-forgiveness!

First off, it's important to forgive yourself for any past hurt or trauma you may have endured. Whether it happened when you were a child, teenager, or adult, please know that you were never responsible for the abuse you faced. You couldn't have done anything to deserve it or make it happen. So, let yourself off the hook and start this journey of self-love with a clean slate!

If you have just come out of a relationship with a narcissist, you're probably feeling especially down on yourself. "I should have gotten out sooner," right? But hey, aren't you forgetting how manipulative narcissists can be? These types of people are expert abusers and know how to keep their victims trapped. They can mess with your head, so it's not your fault for not noticing the warning signs or struggling to leave. So, don't blame yourself for any of it.

Forgive yourself for any actions you may have taken to protect yourself or deal with past abuse too. Remember, you were just trying to survive a tough situation and it wasn't your fault. If you're struggling to forgive yourself, consider how holding onto that guilt impacts you in the present.

You have already learned how to spot narcissists and their tactics now. So, instead of dwelling on the past, focus on what you can do right now to make positive changes in your life. Take the time to heal and develop your strengths with kindness and courage. Your experience with a narcissist has taught you valuable lessons that you can use in future relationships. Beating yourself up won't change anything. You can't change the past or know what would have happened if you had made different choices.

Don't get stuck in a cycle of self-blame. The narcissist is the one responsible for their abusive behavior, and you didn't deserve it. It's time to work on letting go and moving toward a happier, more loving future!

Grow your trust in yourself.

In a healthy relationship, both people strive to grow and improve together. However, in a narcissistic and abusive relationship, you may constantly adjust and compromise until you completely lose sight of who you are. You start to doubt your own feelings because you have been dismissed and invalidated so often. You also start to feel overly responsible for things that are not your fault. Your friend or partner may have blamed you for things you could not have controlled, leading you to feel guilty and ashamed.

Finally, you start to believe that you are somehow inferior to other people and automatically take a backseat in relationships. This can be incredibly damaging to your self-esteem and make it difficult to build healthy connections with others.

As you navigate through life, it is important to rely on both the opinions of others and your intuition. But narcissistic abuse, with how you have been controlled, belittled, manipulated, dismissed, and mocked, makes it hard for you to trust yourself. The balance becomes disrupted and you either become overly dependent on other people's opinions or start to excessively rely solely on your intuition because you can't trust anyone else.

The narcissist may have made you feel this way, but now you have all the control you should have over your life. Learn to listen to your inner voice, and then learn to trust it. Who says you can't be trusted when it's the narcissist who messed up and lied to you and everyone else around you? Didn't your gut feeling start telling you that something was wrong? So, reconnect with your inner wisdom and find that balance again. Start trusting yourself again.

Feel your feelings. Even the uncomfortable ones.

When you were in a relationship with a narcissist, it was hard to express your feelings in a safe way. When you felt angry or sad, the narcissist might have responded in a hurtful manner or even made fun of you. When you felt excited or happy, they also criticized you, didn't they? Narcissists love to interfere with your emotions because they don't know how to deal with their own.

They disrupt your emotions, your relationships, and even your goals. Anything that you felt passionately about was at risk of being criticized. So, what did you do in response? You might have developed the habit of shutting down to protect yourself. If so, you may have lost touch with your emotions and struggle to express them.

Healing from this kind of abuse involves reconnecting with your feelings safely.

Give yourself permission to feel emotions like anger and rage. These are normal and understandable responses to any difficult experiences you may have endured. You have to acknowledge that your parent, friend, or partner with narcissistic tendencies fell short, and feeling frustrated or upset with them is okay. Remember, this doesn't make you a bad person and it won't hinder your ability to love yourself or others.

While it's important to release any pent-up anger and allow yourself to grieve for what you've lost, connecting with emotions that make you feel good is also important. So, allow yourself to laugh out loud at your own jokes or take a moment to appreciate the beauty of nature too. It's okay to feel hopeful and love yourself!

Set your boundaries.

While setting boundaries is an important part of healthy relationships, it is also a way to show love to yourself. Boundaries help you know your limits, define them, and communicate them with others around you. When you set healthy boundaries, you are able to interact and connect with others while showing accountability and compassion from both sides.

You heal when you realize that your needs are important. Healing also means taking responsibility for yourself. You have the power to choose who you spend your time with, and setting boundaries can also help reduce stress and frustration. You can surround yourself with positive and supportive people by creating space for yourself.

It may not seem like it at the moment, but you have the power to make positive changes in your life. You can redefine your boundaries whenever you're ready and take charge of your happiness and healing. The best part is that it's all about you!

Celebrate!

Celebrate your accomplishments, no matter how small they may seem! It's important to develop a habit of positive self-talk by acknowledging and jotting down your daily achievements. It's worth celebrating even if it's just brushing your teeth or standing up for yourself. So, give yourself a pat on the back and maybe even reward yourself with something. You're doing great!

Be kind to yourself. Use kind words.

Instead of beating yourself up over things, why not try talking to yourself like you would a dear friend? Think about it: Would your best friend ever put you down for not feeling happy all the time? Of course not! They would probably give you a hug and ask what they could do to help. So, why can't you do that for yourself? It's not weird, selfish, weak, or vain at all. Just give it a shot!

Give yourself time.

In a healthy relationship, time is a precious gift that is shared between two people who cherish each other. However, in an emotionally abusive relationship, time is often used as a tool to manipulate and control you. Narcissists want to tie your attention, affection, and efforts solely to them, but that is not how a loving relationship should be.

You may have experienced being told who you can or cannot hang out with or being made to feel like your passions and dreams are a waste of time. This kind of behavior is not okay, and it is not a reflection of your worth. Leaving an abusive and narcissistic relationship is definitely scary, and it's normal to feel lost and uncertain about what comes next. But you have the power to take back control of your life and live it in a way that brings you peace and satisfaction. Take all the time you need and don't rush your healing.

No matter how the narcissistic abuse has affected you, healing is possible with no set deadline. Take care of yourself in your own way. Do something that makes you happy, like adopting a pet or moving to a new city to pursue your dream. It's your time; you only get to decide how to use it.

Discovering how to love yourself can be a challenging step on your path to healing, but it's also one of the most crucial acts of self-care you can give yourself. You are definitely worth it, believe me. And I promise you, it will get easier as you keep practicing.

Leaving a narcissistic abuser is a huge step toward a happier and healthier life. It's now time for you to experience all the joy and fulfillment that life has to offer. To heal from the abuse, focus on increasing your self-love. Remember that during the abuse, you were treated poorly and it's time to start treating yourself with kindness and care. This is all about reclaiming your true self and living your best life!

Abuse Blindness

Of course, you now feel like you had been so caught up in your new relationship that you didn't see the warning signs of your narcissistic partner and friend. But you know what? That's totally normal. That's how all victims feel before they realize they've been trapped. It can be easy to miss those red flags when certain traits or dynamics blind us. And it's nothing to beat ourselves over! We did nothing wrong now, did we?

There are many reasons for someone to grow blind to abuse, but the most significant one is that we're not educated on narcissism and how it manifests. Even if we were, it's still pretty hard to recognize the signs and tactics until you're deeply involved with them. And, well, by that time, you'd also realize that you're already trapped.

However, if you read up on it extensively and pay attention to your surroundings, you could probably spot an abusive or toxic person after a few interactions with them. Sometimes, some potential victims trust their gut feeling and keep themselves away from the narcissist, while others just can't identify what feels wrong and just fall for the narcissist's love bombing. Neither of these people is in the wrong or to blame, but what really makes the latter blind to abuse?

Here are some common traits that can make it hard for you to spot a narcissistic partner:

You don't know how to recognize the abuse.

Of course, if you don't know how to differentiate an abusive relationship from a healthy relationship, you can't tell if your partner or abuser is a narcissist. You wouldn't even realize the abuse that was happening. Maybe it feels familiar or even like love. Maybe you believe your relationship with your spouse is great, for example, just because you feel you are compatible in the bedroom.

But if you dig deeper, you will realize that they are actually very controlling and abusive. Only when you uncover the root of your unstable emotions do you realize the abuse you have been enduring. How does this happen? It could be because you have been exposed to this kind of behavior to the point that it has been normalized for you.

Your parents or guardians, your siblings, or even your childhood friend could have been abusive to you to the point that you see such behavior as normal. So, when a narcissist treats you the same way, you don't realize that you are being abused. It may feel like love to you, but it's abuse and never okay.

You're used to following strict rules and obeying others.

Do you find yourself being comfortable or familiar with following strict guidelines? It's possible that your upbringing or cultural background had certain expectations that you felt obligated to fulfill. Maybe you didn't have the freedom to choose your own path or beliefs and instead had to conform to the expectations of your family or community. Love may have seemed conditional, where you had to meet certain criteria to be accepted.

So, when someone new enters your life and sets their own rules, it feels familiar and normal. You see nothing wrong with it because that's how you've been raised.

You are only appreciated for your potential to make someone else happy.

When children don't feel loved, they often try to earn it in any way they can. They become a distraction, a source of happiness, or even try to be less of a burden. Everything they do revolves around one question: "Am I lovable yet?" or "Am I good enough for them?"

Now, imagine meeting a charming, successful person who shows interest in you. It's natural to feel valued and appreciated, even if the relationship is one-sided. Your job is to fulfill their needs and desires, and it's only through their praise and attention that you feel validated. If they stop giving you consistent affirmation, it can leave you wondering, "Am I not good enough anymore?"

You subconsciously put the blame on yourself and never consider the idea that maybe the other person is not good enough for you.

You are a very responsible person.

One way to identify someone who is responsible is if they take on a lot of tasks and duties. They know what they are responsible for and how to take responsibility for things they have done. Conversely, those with narcissistic tendencies always avoid taking responsibility for their actions and feel unappreciated. So, these people seek out victims who are highly responsible. Why? To shift all the blame onto them since the latter are used to taking responsibility for things.

If you are a person who has a lot of responsibilities in life, the narcissist will pick you out to shift even theirs on you. They don't like to take accountability for their actions, but you do. Think about it: in situations where the narcissist feels slighted, they can quickly shift blame onto you, causing you, as the responsible person, to question your own abilities.

You are a bit naïve.

If you've grown up in challenging or even dangerous circumstances, it can make you extra cautious of people's intentions. You learn to be aware that not everyone has pure motives, and this can actually help you recognize signs of narcissism in others. However, if you have had a more sheltered upbringing and haven't encountered people who don't have your best interests at heart, you may not be as quick to spot problematic behavior. You might be more likely to fall for the idea that you're needed and rush in to help or fix things.

Recognizing manipulation, especially when it's directed at you, takes a certain level of life experience and emotional maturity. There's nothing wrong with being pure and trusting of others; it's actually a good trait, but it also makes you vulnerable and easy to target from an abuser's viewpoint.

You tend to ignore your gut feelings.

Have you ever had a feeling that something was off in a relationship, but you ignored it? Maybe you thought you were being too sensitive or that it was all in your head. Well, let me tell you, it happens to the best of us! Perfectionism and shame can make us feel stuck and keep us from acknowledging red flags. But there's a reason why they say you should always trust your gut!

If you have a feeling that there's something wrong, there probably is. Maybe you've experienced situations where your gut feeling was wrong, but that doesn't mean it's going to be the case every time and that you should stop trusting yourself. After all, it's better to be safe than sorry!

Empaths & Narcissists – A Dynamic Duo

In a dynamic between a narcissist and an empath, the balance can often tilt in favor of one person, resulting in an imbalanced give and take. The best word to describe such a relationship would be "parasitic" because the empath genuinely wants to offer care and affection to the narcissist, while the latter only wants to control the empath. It is very common for narcissists to take advantage of empaths due to their inclination toward emotional manipulation and self-centeredness.

We know what a narcissist is, but an empath? Well, these are people who possess an incredible ability to connect with the emotions of those around them, having a special sensitivity toward others' feelings. They naturally place the needs of others before their own, generously giving without even having to be asked. They are the exact opposites of narcissists who only care for themselves.

So, why are narcissists and empaths attracted to each other?

Empaths and narcissists have a special connection, as empaths have a natural desire to help, heal, support, and satisfy others, which perfectly complements the emotional requirements of narcissists. On the other hand, narcissists can manipulate empaths to ignite their natural desire in question. This dynamic is what connects them, and attracts them like magnets, as one wants to give and the other wants to take – even though, in the end, the relationship will still be toxic and unhealthy.

You might also have stayed in an abusive relationship because you feel ashamed that you hadn't recognized the signs earlier. But the truth is, these dynamics can happen in any relationship, not just with a narcissist. It's not always easy to forgive yourself and move on, especially when you feel like you've made a mistake. You might even try to make the relationship look perfect, but that's not always possible.

The good news is that you can learn from your mistakes and be more aware of your blind spots in the future. Don't beat yourself up over past choices; instead, use them as a lesson moving forward. Start loving yourself and being kind to yourself. Healing is not a linear journey, neither is it a destination, so give yourself all the time and love you need.

Remember, ultimately it was you who chose to live a better life by leaving the relationship behind, and that's pretty awesome! It wasn't a walk in the park, but you made it happen. This process of rediscovering self-love takes time, so be patient with yourself and celebrate every little victory along the way. You're doing great!

CHAPTER 10:

THE SURVIVORS JOURNEY

Experiencing narcissistic abuse can be a truly disorienting and devastating ordeal that leaves you feeling drained and depleted on every level. Even though it may not always involve physical harm, the toll it takes on a person's body and mind is no less as it is still incredibly serious. Sadly, victims often struggle to find the support they need, as the damage can be difficult to detect from the outside. You can't see the emotional wounds and the hurt that has been inflicted on them. So, victims are left feeling trapped and alone, struggling to escape the isolation that surrounds them.

Navigating the journey to freedom can be awfully challenging, especially when those we once trusted question our experiences and dismiss our struggles. But with a strong support system and a commitment to our own well-being, we can rise above the chaos and reclaim joy and peace.

This is what the journey of a victim to a survivor looks like:

Feeling that something isn't quite right.

It's easy to miss the signs of dealing with a narcissist or experiencing narcissistic abuse, but the first step toward healing often starts with a gut feeling that things aren't quite right in the relationship. You might have a sense that you're being treated unfairly or that something just feels off, especially after a disagreement. But it's also quite common to dismiss these thoughts and carry on with the unhealthy relationship.

Sometimes, people whom narcissist has abused can have moments where they start to see that what the narcissist is doing is not okay. But it's not always easy to accept that someone you care about could be treating you badly. Some people may try to make excuses for the narcissist, like saying they're having a bad day or going through a tough time. They might even point out times when the narcissist was really kind to them. If you do that, you would be forcing yourself to ignore the 10 bad things they did to just focus on the 1 good they did! In the end, you're gaslighting yourself as the narcissist has always done.

This is a normal part of the journey, and it's okay to take your time getting to a place where you can see things clearly. Remember, healing is a journey, not a destination.

Not being able to ignore the abuse anymore.

At some point in the future, the level of narcissism or mistreatment may reach a point where it becomes challenging to ignore or deny. Acknowledging that someone you love may be a narcissist or that you are experiencing abuse can be a tough pill to swallow. It can be a jarring experience that causes confusion and cognitive dissonance, but it's important to remember that seeking help and support is always an option. You start to get that nagging feeling that something just isn't right, but still find yourself resisting that realization. That inner conflict can be tough to navigate, especially when it comes to dealing with narcissists.

It's a natural response to go back and forth between blaming them and blaming yourself. But eventually, with time and self-reflection, you will come to a place of acceptance and move on to the next phase. Just remember, taking the time you need to process and grow from these experiences is okay.

Accepting the narcissist's true identity.

As time goes on and you start to reflect on your relationship more, there comes a moment of clarity where you finally realize that your loved one is, in fact, a narcissist and an abuser. This realization may come after doing some research on narcissism or talking to a trusted friend about the situation. It's a hard realization to come to, but it's also a crucial turning point. Once you've acknowledged and labeled the abuse, ignoring it or pretending it's not happening becomes much harder.

It's not uncommon for people to hold onto hope that the narcissist in their life can transform, heal, and cease their harmful behavior. You may even have attempted to mend the relationship by turning to therapy or encouraging the narcissist to do so. Unfortunately, that doesn't help in most cases - a narcissist would either refuse to accept there's something wrong with them or make you believe that you are the one who needs to fix their behavior. Eventually, your efforts will not lead to the desired outcome.

Now, you would have no choice but to progress to the next phase of parting ways with the abuser. Remember, prioritizing your well-being is always important; there is nothing wrong with seeking support during difficult times.

Gathering the courage to leave.

After some time, and a bit more abuse from the narcissist, you come to the realization that the narcissistic person in their life is not capable or willing to change. It's then up to you, as the survivor, to gather the strength to move forward. This could involve taking a break from the relationship or simply limiting contact with the narcissist.

Now, we know what happens here. The abuser will most likely respond with love bombing, rage, or even more abuse. That is when you have to realize that it's best to sever ties and completely end your relationship. This will, of course, be very challenging and stressful, particularly for those who have deep connections or had children with their abuser. The narcissist might react harshly and vindictively, causing harm to the survivor, or using alternate methods to retaliate.

Dealing with emotional wounds.

Feeling a rollercoaster of emotions when healing from narcissistic abuse after a breakup is natural. You may experience complicated grief or complex post-traumatic stress disorder, making navigating through your feelings tough. Unlike a typical mourning process, complicated grief can cause you to feel a range of emotions such as anger, guilt, and sadness all at once. These complex emotions can make it hard to process your loss, accept that your relationship with the narcissist is no longer there, and ultimately find closure. Remember, it's okay to take the time you need to heal and work through these emotions with the support of loved ones.

When dealing with a narcissist, it's also okay to feel overwhelmed by emotions. Unfortunately, these feelings can be exacerbated by the fear of what the narcissist may do next to hurt you. Ideally, the best situation is when the narcissist just cuts ties with you completely and ceases all contact, but this can make it difficult to process your emotions and move on.

Sadly, because of their emotional and social limitations, having a clean break from a narcissist is nearly impossible. But don't worry, there are ways to heal and move forward from this tough situation.

Educating and empowering yourself.

If you have recently ended a relationship with someone who was abusive and narcissistic, you'll know it is a tough road to recovery. As you finally break free from the narcissist's hold, what you can do is educate yourself. Education can be a big help. You can turn to self-help books and support groups that are there to offer you insight and understanding. By learning more about narcissism and narcissistic abuse, you can gain some clarity and feel more empowered moving forward.

You can also try keeping a journal of any incidents that occur, including dates and details about what happened. This can help you recognize patterns and behaviors and ultimately aid in your recovery process.

Research can also be a great way for people to connect with others who have gone through similar experiences with narcissistic abuse. It's amazing how validating it can be to find others who understand what you've been through! And this kind of research can really help you find the support you need to recover and make sense of the abuse you've experienced.

By empowering yourself through this process, you can find the closure you need to move forward and heal. So, don't be afraid to reach out and connect with others who have been there before – they may be the key to your full recovery! You're already on the journey to recovery as understanding narcissism comes first.

Healing and practicing self-love.

The journey's next step is finding what makes you happy and helps you heal from the pain of your past. It's time to focus on yourself and reconnect with your own feelings, wants, and needs. This includes practicing self-love and prioritizing self-care. Trust me, you deserve nothing but the best, so put yourself first and start exploring the skills and support that will help you thrive!

Narcissists always put themselves first and don't care about how others feel. It is pretty hurtful, and sometimes, it even makes us forget about our own feelings and needs. So, now it's time for you to take care of yourself and learn to acknowledge and honor your own emotions and needs. Treat yourself with love, respect, and lots of care.

Rebuilding your life.

Narcissists tend to influence others to spend a lot of time and effort on meeting their needs, which makes the victims neglect their own. Additionally, they often come across as bossy, demanding to know everything about what you do, how you act, where you visit, and whom you spend time with. Thus, it is not uncommon for you to develop codependent patterns that can be tough to break free from.

One key step in the healing journey is rebuilding a life that's truly your own. This means figuring out what YOU want, need, care about and building a meaningful life around those things. It's not always easy, but it's definitely worth it!

One way to start fresh is by learning something new. Returning to school, trying out a new career, or pursuing a hobby you've always been interested in are great ways to boost your confidence and self-esteem. Another important step is surrounding yourself with supportive people. Be around people who lift you up and treat you with respect. Building healthy relationships is key to moving on from past hurts and finding happiness in the present.

So, don't be afraid to reach out, make new friends, and reconnect with old ones.

Learning more from the abuse.

By the time we reach this part of the journey, we may start feeling like we've patched up our emotional wounds. The grief and struggles that once hindered us from moving forward no longer seem to have a hold over our daily lives. Some people even find this to be the end of their healing journey, and that's okay. But for others, there's a yearning to take things further. For them, the next step could be discovering a purpose or finding meaning from the pain they've experienced.

Acknowledging the ways in which a past experience made us stronger or wiser doesn't necessarily mean we're happy about what happened or thankful for the relationship that caused it. It's simply recognizing the silver lining and how it has positively impacted our lives. For instance, some people find that recovery helps them cultivate better boundaries, deeper self-awareness, and even self-love.

Moving forward as a helper.

As you progress in your journey and go from a victim to a survivor, you can take more steps to survive and thrive from the abuse. One way to do this is by spreading positivity and sharing your experience. You can do this by lending a helping hand to others who are going through similar experiences or by using your own story to inspire and motivate others. You can also start your very own support group, providing resources to victims and survivors to empower them and help them heal from narcissistic abuse. It's all about making a difference!

You can also make a difference in your unique and intimate way. Maybe you can teach valuable lessons and educate your kids about maintaining healthy boundaries and relationships. Or you can lend a listening ear and offer your unwavering support to a friend who may be struggling in an abusive relationship.

If you feel comfortable, you can also share your own experiences with those who are going through similar situations. It can be a pleasant way to find closure and move on after experiencing narcissistic abuse.

Why do narcissists love to victimize themselves?

Even though some narcissists come across as confident and self-assured, they can actually be quite vulnerable and easily influenced. It's important to remember that we all have our weaknesses and it's okay to admit them. However, narcissists have a tendency to victimize themselves by avoiding accountability and not taking action to solve problems, which could stem from them having low self-esteem.

Have you ever wondered, though, why they seem to always see themselves as a victim? Well, it turns out that those who have a victim mentality may have faced some tough times or trauma in the past but simply haven't learned how to cope in a healthier way. This can lead to a negative outlook on life, where they feel like they have no control over what happens to them.

While feeling down when things don't go as planned is natural. Constantly wallowing in self-pity is never good. Some people with narcissistic tendencies may use this as a way to feel like a hero - a misunderstood and mistreated protagonist in their own story. However, this inflated sense of self-worth isn't genuine and can leave them feeling unsatisfied. By playing the victim, they try to convince themselves and others that their needs should come first.

Remember that even if the narcissist may have gone through terrible times as a child, their difficult childhood doesn't excuse abusive behavior later on in life. We all can change and grow into better versions of ourselves!

Narcissists also have a way of making you feel guilty for not taking their side in a disagreement. Since they are portraying themselves as the victim and as the "good" person, of course, you would be the "bad" one for going against them. It's natural to want to make things right and avoid conflict, but you don't have to compensate or agree to things you're not comfortable with just to ease your guilt. Narcissistic thinking can be very extreme, as we talked about their splitting behavior which makes it impossible to find a middle ground, and it's okay to stand up for yourself.

Narcissists also find solace in the spotlight. Assuming the role of a victim can elicit compassion and empathy from others, which will lead to them gaining a lot of support and encouragement from others. Unfortunately, this approach can also result in unfounded accusations and unwarranted blame directed toward you, making it challenging to navigate the situation.

And when you find yourself in such a difficult situation with a narcissist, it is never easy or effective to communicate your thoughts and feelings. They usually just turn the tables on you, making it seem like you're the one in the wrong. This can make it even more challenging to express yourself and stand up for yourself in the relationship. Even when you try to address issues with them, they respond in a way that puts you on the defensive.

This can be really frustrating, but it's important to remember that it's not your fault. No matter what they say or force you to believe, only listen to yourself and trust yourself. In the end, the narcissist will try and get you to apologize, even when you've done nothing wrong.

Just remember, you're not the villain just because you don't agree with them.

Never forget that you are a unique and special being. The narcissist may have been mean and hurtful to you, but you don't have to treat yourself the same way. How you think and speak about yourself matters a lot because your words and thoughts have a lot of power - you can manifest your dreams!

Change can be scary, but try to approach it with an open heart and remember that you are strong and adaptable. Trust the journey, even if it gets tough. And when you're feeling down, reflect on how amazing you are and all the positive things you've accomplished. Go ahead and experience new and exciting things, and don't be afraid to break away from anything that's been holding you back.

Narcissistic abuse can be very sneaky. It can really take a toll on a person's self-esteem. But don't worry, and it's totally possible to recover and heal from this kind of trauma! Of course, it can be a bit of a journey to get there, but with a great support system and a bit of awareness, you can do it! Just keep reminding yourself that you are incredible and capable of handling anything that comes your way.

Believe in yourself and TRUST THE JOURNEY - even though it may be tough at times. Whenever you feel drained, take a moment to remember how amazing you are and how far you've come. Embrace new experiences and let go of anything that's been holding you back. You've got this!

CHAPTER 11:

PHYSICAL AND MENTAL EFFECTS OF NARCISSISTIC ABUSE

We are now aware that there are many different ways that narcissistic abuse can present itself. It could be verbal, physical, emotional, or sexual - which is why it's tough to define and even harder to understand its short- and long-term effects. But with the increased knowledge of the common tactics used by narcissists to control their victims, we are now ready to delve into the lasting impact that this kind of abuse can have on a person's mental and emotional health.

And hey, don't worry, if you're someone who has experienced narcissistic abuse, there is hope! I'll be offering some guidance on how to recover and move forward from this difficult situation.

In the world of dealing with narcissists, let's think of the term "**physiological terrorism**" to describe the impact they can have on our feelings and well-being. Picture it like this: a narcissist is someone who consistently and intentionally plays with our emotions, leaving us feeling down about ourselves. They do this by disregarding our feelings, constantly craving praise, and acting as if they deserve it all. This hurtful behavior isn't just in our minds - it

149

can actually cause stress and anxiety, affecting us mentally and physically. In simpler terms, dealing with narcissists can really throw a wrench in our happiness and health by being unkind and self-centered.

It's important to recognize that those experiencing narcissistic abuse may be going through a really challenging time. The effects can be incredibly difficult to deal with emotionally and physically. Unfortunately, victims often struggle with post-traumatic stress disorder, anxiety, depression, and even thoughts of hurting themselves. The abuse can appear in physical forms like chronic pain, digestive problems, and frequent headaches.

What's worse, the long-term effects can seriously impact your sense of self-worth and leave you feeling so helpless and powerless that you sometimes don't even consider seeking help or support from outside. This is why it's so important to remember to support those around us who may be dealing with this situation and offer them a listening ear and a helping hand.

This is what we call learned helplessness. It's when you convince yourself that the abuse will continue to happen, that there's no way out, and that you can't do anything to get out. It's a condition that can develop in people who have experienced narcissistic abuse. Essentially, you start to believe that you have no power to make positive changes in your life. This can be tough to deal with, as it can make you feel like you're forever stuck in a bad situation you can't escape.

As time passes, you start to feel even more hopeless and worthless, which can hurt your self-esteem and sense of self. But you know what? You're not alone in dealing with this too! There is help available, and you can take steps to regain your sense of power and control.

So, the first effect of narcissistic abuse on a victim is:

Lack of Self-Worth and Self-Esteem

If you've never experienced narcissistic abuse firsthand, imagine living with someone who constantly belittles you and makes you feel like you're always wrong. It might seem like a situation you can easily get out of, but if you've been made to believe things that are not true and make you look like you're in the wrong, that could really lead you to doubt your own worth. Unfortunately, such toxic relationships are very real, and this is a common tactic used by narcissists to gain control over their victims.

The long-term effects of this type of emotional abuse can be devastating. Before you realize it, you'll have fallen to extremely low self-esteem and feelings of unworthiness. Of course, when you are repeatedly told that you are not good enough, it's normal to find it hard to believe in yourself and your abilities.

But remember, again, that you are not to be blamed for the abuse you have endured and that there is always hope for healing and rebuilding your self-esteem.

151

Lack of Energy

Feeling constantly tired and lacking both emotional and physical energy is not only a sign that something isn't right, but it's also a serious warning that you're either being abused or have an underlying physical illness.

If you're in a relationship with a narcissist, their draining behavior can leave you feeling exhausted. It's important to listen to your body and seek help if you're experiencing chronic fatigue. A proper diagnosis can help uncover the root cause of your exhaustion and allow you to start feeling better. Don't hesitate to reach out for support!

Post-Traumatic Stress

After going through narcissistic abuse, it's quite common to start encountering post-traumatic stress symptoms. Your mind becomes hyper-vigilant, constantly scanning for potential threats around you. This heightened state is a natural response to the trauma that you have experienced in the relationship. Being with a narcissist activates your fight or flight mode, where your instinct tells you to either fight or flee - and sometimes, freeze. You naturally develop this extreme sense of caution due to the abuse you have endured.

A lot of victims express concern that they never knew what their narcissistic abuser would do in different situations. You never know when they are going to lash out at you. Their behavior is completely unpredictable, so all you can do is stay persistently vigilant at all times. You find it difficult to unwind and constantly anticipate their presence. Your brain then naturally goes into fight or flight mode to respond to the trauma and perceived threat or danger.

Consequently, anything that reminds you of those distressing memories can potentially lead to anxiety episodes. This is why you may choose to distance yourself from certain places, situations, people, and triggers that remind you of the abuse. You may start avoiding specific people and locations that evoke those painful memories.

Frequent Panic Attacks

Dealing with a narcissistic partner can really take a toll on your mental condition. Stress and panic attacks are often common responses to their demanding and pressurizing behavior. Feeling like you're constantly in danger of doing or saying something wrong is easy. And because you never know when the narcissist will attack you again, you always feel anxious and stressed. That's how panic attacks develop. But remember, you don't have to suffer in silence. Relationships should make you feel calm, safe, and happy.

Memory Problems

Dealing with narcissistic abuse can make it hard for you to focus on things or even remember important stuff. You might find it tough to stay focused on your daily routine, even if it's something as simple as watching TV or scrolling through social media. Recollections of traumatic incidents can disrupt your ability to concentrate and pay attention. You may also find yourself struggling with forgetfulness, particularly with short-term memories. This is because your brain produces more stress hormones when it undergoes trauma, which can impact how your mind stores and remembers your memories.

Loss of Trust in Others

It's not uncommon to have trust issues after experiencing emotional abuse, especially if it came from a narcissist, but it's important to remember that it doesn't have to define your future relationships. While it's natural to be cautious, we should try not to let past experiences hinder our ability to connect with others.

You might find yourself taking a bit longer to trust people, and that's okay. It's important to take the time to build relationships at your own pace and be open about your concerns. Of course, it will not be easy to stop doubting others and wondering if they are out to manipulate you too, but sometimes you just have to give people the benefit of the doubt. It's hard to trust even your closest friends when the narcissist who was equally as close to you ends up abusing and mistreating you. We couldn't really tell they would turn out this way, and we actually liked them in the beginning. So, we start doubting everyone who is nice to us in fear that they may turn out to be a narcissist too.

Declining Mental Health

Naturally, the toxic and abusive tactics used by narcissists are bound to cause extreme damage to your mental health. It's actually quite common for victims to develop anxiety and depression as a result. You may constantly feel on edge or stressed, and even lose interest in things you once loved. This is not easy to deal with and can leave you feeling even more hopeless and worthless like you don't deserve to be loved or respected. These feelings are valid, but please seek support so you can heal and move forward.

Other psychological impacts include unresolved trauma that can make it hard for you to trust others and build healthy, trusting relationships. In more extreme cases, it's not uncommon to develop PTSD or CPTSD, which can be even more debilitating. If you're experiencing any of the symptoms of post-traumatic stress disorder, such as flashbacks, nightmares, anxiety, or depression, please know that you're not alone and there is help.

Relationship Problems

Dealing with a narcissist also impacts on your relationships, causing strain and even leading to problems with friends and family. Living in constant fear and anxiety, always walking on eggshells, can create resentment and anger over time. And this is not only limited to your relationship with the narcissist but also those around you. Apart from narcissists' tactics to keep you away from your family and friends, you isolate yourself or create misunderstandings from your unstable emotional condition.

In any case, it's not your fault. You're living under constant pressure and anxiety, which only makes it understandable that you have a hard time dealing with other relationships. The good news is that help is available! Don't hesitate to contact a therapist or other professional service for guidance and assistance. Remember, there's no shame in seeking support; it can make all the difference in improving your relationships and overall well-being.

Unhealthy Coping Mechanisms

Another possible outcome of surviving narcissistic abuse is the development of unhealthy and destructive behavior. Sometimes, victims who have experienced this type of abuse feel so guilty or responsible for their partner's mistreatment of them that they start showing self-destructive patterns to cope with it. This includes addictive behaviors like substance use, overeating, and overspending.

The victim just sees those as a means of coping with their emotional turmoil. It's the exact opposite of self-love and self-care that are key to healing and actually help in overcoming these challenges.

Physical Health Impacts

Like your emotional and mental health, a toxic relationship can also have physical effects on your body. Essentially, the extreme mental effects cause physical problems in the long run. Chronic pain, digestive issues, and headaches are just a few examples. This is because when you're stressed out all the time, your body produces a hormone called cortisol. If cortisol levels remain high for too long, it can really take a toll on your health.

Our physical health can be heavily influenced by our emotional and psychological well-being. This means that when you experience things like narcissistic abuse can have serious implications on your physical health and well-being. Your body is constantly sending you messages, and it's always trying to communicate with you. When something isn't quite right, your body often lets you know through various symptoms and sensations. So, always pay attention to it.

When you've been living with an abusive and narcissistic partner for a long time, you experience physical changes like feeling less hungry, having trouble sleeping, tiredness, or having digestive issues. It's important to remember that abuse can be sneaky and not always easy to spot, even for those who are watching closely. But your body is incredibly intuitive and responsive to the environment and experiences around you!

Narcissistic abuse can have a range of negative impacts on your health. Some common physical symptoms of narcissistic abuse include headaches, digestive issues, muscle tension, chronic pain, and fatigue. These symptoms are often a result of the stress and anxiety caused by the abuse. It's crucial for you to listen to your body and seek help if you're experiencing any of these symptoms. Remember, it's never too late to prioritize your health and well-being. Your body doesn't lie and it's important to take care of yourself both emotionally and physically.

Victims of narcissistic abuse often live in constant fear, anxiety, and uncertainty, which can be very unsettling and confusing. The abuse can leave you feeling powerless and helpless, leading to feelings of despair and extreme sadness. So, a lot of victims of abuse hesitate to seek help. But do you really want to spend the rest of your life walking on eggshells all the time because you never know what will happen next? Because you never know when the next attack will happen? This can lead to long-term psychological impacts, such as unresolved trauma and difficulty forming trusting relationships. It can be really tough, and in extreme cases, victims of narcissistic abuse can develop PTSD or CPTSD, which can be extremely debilitating.

Time for some good news now: You can recover from both the mental and physical effects of narcissistic abuse! The first step is to seek support and help. You can start by reaching out to your family and friends, rekindling those connections that the narcissist may have damaged. Various organizations and hotlines are available to provide you with the necessary information and resources, and you can find support groups online or in your local community where you can meet people who have gone through similar experiences.

Furthermore, you could also seek professional help from a therapist or counselor who specializes in narcissistic abuse.

Therapy can be an excellent tool to help you heal and move past the trauma of narcissistic abuse. Talking with a therapist can be a great way to gain an understanding of what you've been through and get guidance on how to move forward. If you're still in the relationship, your therapist can suggest strategies for reducing contact and creating boundaries.

There's no doubt that dealing with the effects of narcissistic abuse, even after you've left the relationship, is incredibly difficult. But with the right support and tools, you can start to heal. Your therapist can help you find coping strategies that work for you and recommend resources to assist in your recovery.

It's also important to take care of yourself during this time. Finding activities that bring you joy and focusing on self-care can help you rebuild your self-esteem and improve your mood. Simple things like eating well and exercising can also make a big difference in how you feel.

While recovering can take some time, remember that the damage isn't permanent. With the right kind of support and guidance, you can absolutely move forward and live your life to the fullest.

CHAPTER 12:

THE ROAD TO HEALING

Going through the aftermath of abuse can be a tough road to navigate. Just leaving the relationship and getting rid of the narcissist in your life can feel like a huge step, and it is one! But that's not where your journey ends. Now, you have to learn to let go of the effects of the abuse and heal from within. And, sometimes, it may seem like there's no light at the end of the tunnel but I want you to know that healing is possible. We can walk together every step of the way.

It takes a lot of bravery, patience, and self-care to recover from trauma, but with a little bit of guidance and support, you can do it. In this chapter, we'll talk about some essential steps you can take to begin your journey of healing. We'll cover everything from processing your emotions to building up your resilience. By following these strategies, you'll be able to regain control of your life, find self-compassion, and start thriving again. So take a deep breath, and let's get started!

If you're ready to begin your journey toward healing, it's important to first recognize and acknowledge the trauma you've experienced. We'll skip through this step because you're already past that now. Understanding how abuse affects your emotional, mental, and physical well-being is a great starting point. This means recognizing symptoms such as anxiety, depression, flashbacks, or nightmares. Since you have already educated yourself on the common symptoms of abuse, you can figure out the complexities of trauma with only a bit more guidance.

You have the most important tools in your hand now. All you have to do is use them to navigate your healing process with confidence and assurance. Remember, you're not alone on this journey; there is always hope for a brighter future.

Here are your next steps:

Self-care, self-care, and self-care.

Taking care of yourself should be at the top of your to-do list! It's crucial for healing and feeling good after the bad has passed. As a survivor, you must focus on your physical, emotional, and spiritual well-being. This can be as simple as going for a walk, practicing yoga, writing in a journal, or doing something you love that brings you happiness. Make self-care a regular part of your routine, and watch as you start feeling more like yourself and taking charge of your life again.

Look for a little backup.

Going through a tough time can be hard to handle, whether a toxic relationship or a stressful situation. But you don't have to do it alone! Having a support network can be a huge help when you're dealing with trauma. Whether it's your close friends, a family member, or a support group you can trust having people around who care about you and your well-being can give you the emotional support you need to get through it. And if you're looking for some extra guidance, a trained therapist or counselor who knows all about trauma can offer you some specialized techniques to help you heal. Don't be afraid to reach out. Trust me, there's always someone who's got your back!

Build resilience.

Did you know that building resilience is a crucial step in the journey toward healing from any kind of abuse or trauma? It means you, as a survivor, have learned to overcome obstacles, discovered your inner strengths, and moved ahead with positivity. If you want to cultivate resilience, consider challenging your negative thoughts with positive ones, setting achievable goals for yourself, finding healthy ways to cope with stress, and celebrating your personal victories along the way. By focusing on your strengths, you'll gradually build resilience and empower yourself to take charge of your life. You can do this!

Try expressive therapy.

Therapies can really help when it comes to dealing with trauma and abuse. There are different types of therapies, but expressive therapies are more fun and creative. They can be a wonderful tool for you on your healing journey. You can choose music therapy, art therapy, or even dance therapy. All of them offer unique ways to express emotions and release stored trauma. By embracing the creative process, you can delve into your experiences, acknowledge your feelings, and feel more confident and empowered. Plus, expressive therapies provide a safe space for working through and shifting traumatic memories. So, why not try it and see how it positively impacts your healing process?

Lastly, forgive and let go.

Forgiving someone does not mean you have accepted that their behavior was okay. It means you have moved forward and don't want to look back again. It's for you, not for them. Many survivors don't realize the power of forgiveness in the beginning. It does sound hard to be able to forgive someone who caused you so much pain but trust me, and it can totally transform your healing journey.

Just remember, forgiving doesn't mean you have to approve or forget the hurt you've experienced. It's more about freeing yourself from the weight of anger and resentment. Take all the time you need. This process is very personal. You'll need to learn self-compassion and work toward acceptance to achieve closure. By letting go of the past, you can enjoy the present fully and live a future full of amazing possibilities. It's worth it!

The power of detachment is no joke. When you're trying to make positive changes in your life, it's the one thing you should keep in your mind. Taking the time to detach from certain people and situations can help you achieve greater self-realization and growth. If you choose to tolerate toxic or abusive behavior in your life, it's what you will get – that's the harsh reality. The way you tolerate things in your life will ultimately determine what you end up with.

It's important to differentiate between how you feel about someone and how they make you feel. These are two distinct things, and it's okay to acknowledge that someone may not be able or willing to show up for you in the way you wish they would. It's not a reflection of your worth or value as a person. It just shows what they see you as. Instead of feeling upset or disappointed, try to focus on the positive. By recognizing someone for who they truly are, you can move forward with a newfound sense of awareness and clarity. So, stay positive, and keep moving forward!

Letting go of people doesn't mean we don't care about them anymore. It actually means we care about ourselves enough to make tough decisions for our own well-being. We believe in honest and healthy relationships that bring us closer to others and encourage growth. Remember to always respect yourself and your worth. Don't let anyone make you feel like you don't matter or that you're not important. Your top priority in life should only be YOU!

The past doesn't define you, so don't let it hold you back. And don't be afraid to trust others – plenty of amazing people are out there. Just be sure to choose wisely when it comes to who you allow access to your life.

It takes a lot of courage to overcome trauma and stand up for what's right. That's why education and a strong support system are so important. That also includes spreading positivity for other victims like you. Share your knowledge and wisdom, and be a source of healing for those in need. People like you make the world a better place by living out their values. And let's not forget that gratitude is a powerful tool for healing.

The power of healing is truly amazing, and those who possess a strong sense of empathy and sensitivity are able to pick up on the subtlest shifts in energy and atmosphere. Mere words or appearances do not easily fool them, and they're able to detect changes in tone of voice, facial expressions, body language, and even the weird vibes that are sometimes present. These people respond to the true intentions behind words and are always ready to lend a helping hand whenever needed. So, let's all take a moment to appreciate these amazing individuals and also strive to spread more positive energy around us!

Sometimes we end up giving our love to the wrong person and we're left thinking, "What a waste of time. They didn't even deserve it." But hey, let's not beat ourselves up over it! The fact that we could love them at all is a beautiful thing. It shows that we have love inside of us, along with kindness, and honesty inside us. It's their loss for not recognising the positivity and genuine affection they could get from you. What's even sadder is that they don't have the ability to love someone like you do. So, don't focus on how others might abuse or have abused your lovely qualities. Instead, focus on the fact that you have them and they make you an amazing person. You are a beautiful human being.

It's amazing how some people come into our lives for a reason, even if it's just for a short while. They bring with them unique perspectives and teach us about different human characteristics. Sometimes, though, there may be misunderstandings or miscommunications in relationships. Some people may even try to shift blame onto others to avoid taking responsibility for their actions. But it's important to remember that true growth and change come from self-reflection and accountability. When we acknowledge our mistakes and work to improve ourselves, we can better love and support our partners. So, always be humble and be open to personal growth so you can create healthy and loving relationships.

Have you noticed how we often get caught up in the good things and overlook the warning signs when it comes to relationships? Maybe that's another reason narcissists are hard to recognize. Instead of fixating on those green flags, let's focus on the red flags too. It's easy to think we're on the right track when all we're chasing after are the supposedly positive signals. It's never a good idea to ignore the warning signs.

It takes time to truly understand something, but education is key. Sometimes, when we step back from a situation and detach ourselves from it, we gain a new perspective and can finally see the truth. We finally get to see what's behind the mask.

Emotional trauma is extremely tough to deal with, but having supportive people around you who care is a game-changer. Even when someone else's actions hurt you, staying kind and empathetic is important. It shows your true character as a person.

Healing after abuse is a unique journey for each person. It's not impossible, but it's not too easy either. With some active effort to process your trauma and develop resilience, you can gradually regain control of your life, rebuild your self-worth, and feel empowered. It's not always easy, but with time, support, and some good self-care practices, you can heal old wounds and create a new, positive story for yourself. So, keep in mind that healing is totally possible and you can, and should live a life full of happiness, love, and fulfillment!

CHAPTER 13:

REALITY & TRUTHS

Living in a state of constant survival mode can be overwhelming. Fortunately, that's not our reality. It's what they are living in. But spending time with a narcissist can be a rollercoaster of emotions. One day may be filled with laughter and joy, while another may be more challenging. It's unpredictable and so confusing, which is why you always feel like you're walking on eggshells. You don't know if today will be one of the good days or the bad ones. You don't know how to act around narcissists because everything about them is unpredictable.

In the end, you are only left wondering why and how the narcissist could seem so appreciative and valued your relationship, only to suddenly cut you off as if you never meant anything to them. And it's probably true that you never did mean anything to them... It's not that easy to throw someone you love and care about aside like nothing. You don't do that to friends, partners, or anyone you cherish.

It can be puzzling when someone changes quickly, especially if they're a narcissist who seems to thrive on unpredictability. It makes you wonder if they enjoy creating chaos to boost their ego.

And why? That's the biggest question. You are hurt but you are even more confused because you would never do that. Because you're not a narcissist. You don't understand why they enjoy chaos and unpredictability so much when both these things give you so much anxiety.

The simple answer is that narcissists love chaos. Because they prioritize their own needs, they may often prefer a bit of excitement. It's during chaotic times that they feel most empowered. They may even create chaos because it's easier to sway others when they're feeling disoriented. When we are stressed, we tend to become more emotional and less rational, making it easier for someone to influence us. We turn our survival mode on, and our emotions start to overshadow logic. And this is exactly where the narcissist wants to trap you – in constant panic and unstable emotions.

This is how logic escapes us and we fail to see the narcissist's abuse and manipulation. And that's when you begin to question your own reality, doubt yourself, and accept whatever the narcissist says or does to you. Only by relying on your inner compass can you stay grounded and avoid getting swept up in someone else's reality. So, while it's important to recognize when others may be manipulating you, it's also important to take care of your own needs and emotions.

Accountability

While you are living with a narcissistic or toxic person, you will always be the bad one, the one in the wrong, and the one who is always at fault. That's because your friend or partner doesn't want to feel guilty or take responsibility for their own actions. They are aware of the kind of treatment that they have shown you, and they just don't want to acknowledge it or take the blame for it. So, who takes the blame then? Simple: it's you.

Remember, a narcissist will never admit they are at fault or did something wrong. It's always someone else. If not you, they will shift the blame onto another person. Their only reality is that they are the victim. They will always be the victim. And you are the one who has to accept their delusions and make it your reality, too. This can be incredibly frustrating and hurtful, but it's not your fault. Neither is it your responsibility to look out for the narcissist or try to help them. In most cases, there's no help for them.

Well, it's true that most narcissists do not realize they have a problem or may not be interested in changing their ways. However, resources and support are available for those who want to become a better person and acknowledge their behavior. I've had the opportunity to learn from diagnosed narcissists myself, but it's important to keep in mind that this is only a small percentage. So, while it may seem like there's no hope for narcissists, there is always potential for growth and change only if they're willing to seek help and work toward positive change.

Healthy relationships encourage you to grow and prioritize self-reflection. You both take accountability for your actions and strive to be better friends or partners. You both build strong and healthy connections with people around you. You both lift each other up and create positivity and support for each other. None of this happens when you're with a narcissist. Even the good things you noticed at the start, the "positive" vibes that pulled you into the relationship, are all gone after you are successfully lured into their traps.

When you finally realize you've been trapped, you begin to question everything. While it's perfectly normal to be curious about a person's behavior, remember to not let that curiosity consume you or turn into an obsession. You don't have to figure out exactly why the narcissist behaves in a certain way. Unfortunately, if you've been in a relationship with a narcissist, it can be easy to get caught up in figuring out their every move. It can come as a huge shock when the person you cared so much for turns out to be a narcissist. Of course, you would want to know why, when, and where everything happened. But remember, it's important to not let that preoccupation take over your life. It won't make a difference knowing everything about them.

They will simply shift all the blame on you with their manipulation skills. If you react negatively to their abusive behavior, they will start acting like the victim. You disrespected them, but haven't they been doing the same? You only realize how poorly you've been treated when their mask begins to slip. And they will still try to turn it around and blame you for our reaction. That's what they are best at. And remember, manipulation is when they blame you for your reaction to their toxic behavior but never discuss the disrespect that triggered you.

You are a wonderful, caring person, which is why the narcissist tried to take advantage of that. They look for people with everything they don't: loving relationships, empathy, and support. To them, you are one of the richest people in the world. You have all the things they crave and are not! And since they don't know how to deal with their emotions or accept that someone could be better than them, they try to pull you down with them. To make you as miserable as they are. When they could have just learned to be more like you. If only they could.

So, it's not your fault that you attract narcissists, but it's a sign that you have so much going for you! You have everything they don't. However, a relationship with a narcissist can leave you doubtful and bewildered. It's like you're in a different world where you can't seem to make sense of their hurtful behavior, even after talking to them about it. It can be exhausting and traumatizing but know that you're not alone. You can break this cycle and find ways to heal from these experiences.

If someone is causing you pain and they know it, yet they continue to do so, it's important to recognize that this is not okay behavior. They are doing it intentionally, ignoring how it is affecting you or damaging your well-being. It's not a reflection of your worth or your value but rather a reflection of your own issues and limitations. Remember that true love and care do not involve hurting someone intentionally. So, don't blame yourself for their actions, and instead, focus on taking care of yourself and surrounding yourself with people who treat you with respect and kindness.

Do you ever find yourself constantly mulling over a situation, wondering why it keeps happening? It's natural to feel that way, but sometimes, we need to take a step back and consider our own role in the situation. Instead of focusing on changing someone else's behavior (which, let's be honest, is pretty much impossible), we need to hold ourselves accountable and take responsibility for our own actions and choices. It's tough to sit with the uncomfortable feeling of being hurt by someone we care about, but we need to remember that we have the power to make positive changes. So, let's believe people when they show us who they are and prioritize taking care of ourselves!

You know, sometimes we all wear masks and it's not always easy to see what's truly going on beneath the surface. But I believe that honesty and authenticity are so important in our relationships. Assuming that you've already seen the person behind that mask they wear out in public, it's time to stop denying and finally accept that there might be something going on that you're not quite acknowledging. Remember, the mask is fake but the person behind it is very real. So, why deny the reality?

The mask is what pulled you closer, and the real person behind it is a monster. There's no way to change or "fix" a monster, so please run away and don't look back! Do not keep a monster in your life. It will seriously only keep hurting you.

Did you know that most narcissists tend to have a small circle of friends? It's kind of ironic, right? Because if you take a closer look, you'll start to see through their facade. Sometimes people choose not to see the truth, but you should know that even these individuals serve a purpose in our lives - even if it is as an enemy.

And remember, sometimes it's necessary to let go of certain people in our lives to prioritise our well-being. But in the end, I truly believe that everyone we come across is there for a reason, even if it's just to teach us something about ourselves.

People with a tendency toward narcissism sometimes struggle with recognizing their own mistakes and taking responsibility for them. They may feel entitled to prioritize their own needs and have a hard time understanding the impact of their actions on others. Sometimes, they even change the facts to fit their own narrative. However, it's important to approach this behavior with empathy and understanding, as they don't even realize the harm they're causing. They can either be a hero or a victim, but never a villain. I have learned to say that it's a bit like them trying to paint a picture of you only to turn out wishy-washy resulting as a water color!

People around these narcissists often find themselves believing whatever they say, especially when they speak with such conviction. It can be difficult to trust our own instincts, even when they're trying to tell us something different. When we can't see any evidence of wrongdoing, it's easy to keep holding onto the image of a good person, even when faced with someone who may not be so kind. So, it's not just you. This behavior is normal. The narcissist is not.

Such situations leave you feeling confused and unsure of yourself, but please know that you did nothing wrong. You are a caring and compassionate person who wanted to help, but these people have their own issues that they need to work through. You can't change them, but you can take care of yourself and focus on what's best for you. Remember, you can't change someone who does not see a problem with their actions and behaviors!

Don't forget that the pain you feel at the end of a relationship, especially an abusive or narcissistic one, does not reflect who you are as a person. You don't have to tolerate any form of abuse. When things don't go as planned and your heart feels broken, it's okay to take some time to heal and process your emotions.

Remember, these experiences are meant to strengthen you and help you become the amazing person you were always meant to be. So, keep your chin up and know that better things are on the horizon. You got this!

CONCLUSION

I firmly believe that we can shape how others treat us, both through the way we treat ourselves and the boundaries we set with others. I have learned that not establishing healthy boundaries from the start leaves us vulnerable to being mistreated and taken advantage of.

When we choose to tolerate unacceptable behavior from narcissists or anyone else in our lives, we're essentially giving them permission to continue treating us poorly. Remembering that we have the power to stand up for ourselves and say no to mistreatment is vital. By continually giving second chances and overlooking bad behavior, we're essentially handing over control of our emotional well-being to others. It's like saying, "Here are the keys to my emotional states; feel free to do as you wish."

When it comes to second chances, it's important to remember that not everyone deserves them. While it's great to believe in the good in people, giving a narcissist a second, third, or fourth chance will end up causing more harm than good. It will destroy you again and again and again. It WILL be worse than before. It will put your peace and happiness at risk. Your heart, soul, body, and entire life will be destroyed again.

Trust me, I know how hard it is. I gave my partner multiple chances, took him back FIVE times, despite being warned about his behavior, and those things did not only happen to me but got worse. More frequent, more unbearable, viler, and more abusive. It took a toll on me in every way possible - mentally, emotionally, physically, and spiritually. I was slowly bleeding to death and just withering away. I had to seek therapy to address the trauma and other consequences that arose from it, including terrifying nightmares and flashbacks.

I advise anyone in a similar situation to stay away if you're no longer with them. It's best to maintain no contact for your own well-being. There's no other way.

Can someone with narcissistic personality disorder change? While there isn't a yes or no answer to that, in most cases, it is better to assume that they won't. Not because they can't change but simply because they don't want to.

Those with a history of PD from childhood have developed defense mechanisms to protect themselves from feeling shame. These defense mechanisms include not taking accountability for their actions and relying on others to provide them with a sense of worth and self-esteem. People with NPD also struggle with overwhelming feelings of self-loathing and shame, making it difficult for them to show love and empathy toward others. Often, they hide their true selves and see others as mere reflections of themselves, using them to prop up their own self-image.

It is next to impossible to change the core traits of NPD, even if a person with this disorder works with a therapist to develop new coping mechanisms and learn to manage their emotions in a healthier way.

You must understand that some people can't change their behavior, especially those with narcissistic tendencies. Of course, this leads to a variety of negative experiences for those around them, like love bombing, humiliation, gaslighting, trauma bonds, financial control, blackmail, legal manipulation, stalking, cyber abuse, sleep deprivation, entrapment, reverse psychology, false accusations, and the use of fear, guilt, and shame to manipulate and control. It can be a confusing and overwhelming situation, and it's understandable to feel lost and disconnected from yourself. Only when you begin to prioritize your well-being and seek support from trusted friends and professionals can you see their true personality, something that can't be changed.

So, how do you deal with a narcissist? You don't. But what if you're already trapped? Already stuck inside their world and don't see a way out yet? In that case, the best approach would be to maintain a calm and composed demeanor, as if you were a solid rock. By remaining emotionally detached and disinterested, you can divert the attention of a narcissist who wishes to manipulate or harm you. Remember, they thrive on drama and your emotions; you give them nothing, and they might just leave you alone.

This technique, known as the "gray rock method," entails minimizing eye contact, providing concise responses, and redirecting your focus toward other matters when engaging with narcissistic, abusive, and toxic people.

According to Elinor Greenberg, a licensed psychologist and Gestalt therapist specialized in borderline, narcissistic, and schizoid adaptations, one possible explanation for abusive behavior is that individuals with narcissistic tendencies may excel in various areas but struggle when it comes to building healthy relationships.

Keep in mind that they don't have ANY respect for you. They see you as a possession and they don't love you; they don't understand the concept of love and they lack empathy. You have to have empathy to love, and they have none! They simply can NOT love you. It's impossible to reason with someone who doesn't see reality and truth, especially when they don't have a sense of empathy and humanity too. But know that if they loved you, they wouldn't destroy you! You do NOT destroy someone you love.

So, let's break it down. Why is it, by definition, The Narcissist... then Me!? Because it's always about them. You are never first, you never were, and you never will be. Narcissists are only driven by their insatiable need for admiration and validation. They believe that the world revolves around them and they are self-centered to the point that it becomes the main point of every situation and every interaction. You never held any importance in their world.

When you entered the narcissist's world, your needs and desires were thrown away. Their ego comes first, their constant need for attention and praise, and their thirst for self-gratification always come first. You are invisible and unimportant to them. You will always come after.

The thing is that we all have the ability to change and grow. Some people do it faster than others, but it's ultimately up to you to decide whether sacrificing your own needs for someone else is worth it. Just remember, you should never compromise on respect and love. A whole and healthy relationship with any person is ultimately having love, trust, respect, loyalty, and kindness. You cannot compromise on that. A relationship is not meant to be one-sided.

Choose You.

PLEASE CONSIDER LEAVING A REVIEW...

Hello, my lovely reader

I really do hope you enjoyed the book. Please take a moment to leave a review.

As an Author, I know how critical reviews are for getting the word out for my work.

When my readers leave reviews on Amazon for my books, it helps others discover my books and decide what is right for them.

It also gives me valuable feedback on what readers enjoyed and what they didn't.

It doesn't have to be too long; just a few words would be immensely helpful.

Please look out for future books in my series.

Thank you so much for your support.

Avery x

https://www.amazon.com/dp/B09THGK7RB

RESOURCES

- National Domestic Violence Hotline – https://www.thehotline.org/resources/narcissism-and-abuse/
- National Dating Abuse Hotline – https://www.loveisrespect.org/
- National Sexual Assault Hotline – https://www.rainn.org/
- Victim Connect (Harassment, Stalking, and Abuse) Helpline – https://victimconnect.org/
- National Helpline for Male Victims – https://1in6.org/

Professionals/Self-Aware Narcissists

- Dr Les Carter – Surviving Narcissism – https://survivingnarcissism.tv/
- Ben Taylor – Raw Motivations – https://www.rawmotivations.com/
- Lee Hammock – Mental Healness – https://mentalhealness.net/
- Anna Runkle – The Crappy Childhood Fairy – https://crappychildhoodfairy.com/
- Karyl McBride – Licensed Marriage and Family Therapist – https://karylmcbridephd.com/

- Dr Rhonda Freeman – Neuropsychologist and a victim of narcissistic abuse – https://neuroinstincts.com/

Social Media Resources

- Love.leaxo – Narcissistic Abuse Specialist on Instagram – Personal Coach
- https://www.instagram.com/love.leaxo/
- Dave Narcissism Survivor - healing.after.a.narcissism -
- https://www.instagram.com/healing.after.a.narcissist/
- Tiara Thomas – Narcissistic Abuse Specialist on Instagram – https://www.instagram.com/theselflovemethod/
- Narcissistic Abuse Community on Reddit – https://www.reddit.com/r/NarcissisticAbuse/
- Dr Ramani Durvasula on YouTube – https://www.youtube.com/c/DoctorRamani
- Danish Bashir on Instagram – https://www.instagram.com/narcabusecoach/
- Cluster B Milkshake on YouTube – https://www.youtube.com/channel/UC7mkAC2N4PqlGqXfBJMyqCA
- The Little Shaman on YouTube – https://www.youtube.com/@thelittleshamanhealing

Support Groups

- Narcissist Abuse Support Group on Facebook – https://www.facebook.com/groups/188681268196044/
- Co-Dependents Anonymous – https://coda.org/
- Narcissistic Abuse Survivors – https://www.narcissisticabusesurvivors.org/
- MyNARA Support Group on Facebook – https://www.facebook.com/groups/1173575726175953/
- Find Local Support Groups – https://narcissistabusesupport.com/narcissist-abuse-support-groups/

Online Therapy Services

- https://www.online-therapy.com/
- https://www.counselling-directory.org.uk/
- https://www.psychologytoday.com/intl
- https://www.betterhelp.com/get-started/
- https://www.goodtherapy.org/

Blogs/Articles

- Narcissistic Personality Disorder – https://outofthefog.website/personality-disorders-1/2015/12/6/narcissistic-personality-disorder-npd

- Narc Wise – Surviving post narcissistic trauma – https://narcwise.com/
- The Aftermath of Loving a Narcissist – https://psiloveyou.xyz/the-last-goodbye-or-how-to-finally-leave-an-abusive-narcissist-383c452000d6
- Diversion Tactics Manipulative Narcissists Use – https://thoughtcatalog.com/shahida-arabi/2016/06/20-diversion-tactics-highly-manipulative-narcissists-sociopaths-and-psychopaths-use-to-silence-you/
- The Gray Rock Method – https://lovefraud.com/the-gray-rock-method-of-dealing-with-psychopaths/
- When It's Time to Go – https://www.domesticshelters.org/articles/faq/when-it-s-time-to-go-part-i#.VRBaLELAIy4
- Legal Guide to Divorcing a Narcissist – https://bartonfamilylaw.com.au/narcissistic-abuse-narcissistic-abuse-personality-disorder/

Online Assessments

- Narcissistic Personality Disorder Test – https://www.psycom.net/narcissistic-personality-disorder-test
- https://welevelup.com/mental-health/narcissist-quiz/

- 100 Point Narcissist Scale – How to Tell If Your Partner is a Narcissist – https://www.thehartcentre.com.au/what-is-narcissism-and-what-is-narcissistic-behaviour/

UK – https://www.amazon.co.uk/dp/B0CQ5QX8L7

USA – https://www.amazon.com/dp/B0CQ5QX8L7

AUE – https://www.amazon.com.au/dp/B0CQ5QX8L7

CAN – https://www.amazon.ca/dp/B0CQ5QX8L7

Printed in Great Britain
by Amazon

40512520R10109